W0415039

Sur le site compagnon

e for English 5e

www.didier-eforenglish.com

Les vidéos

Les audios

- Réécoute les documents audio découverts en classe
- Regarde à nouveau, avec ou sans sous-titres, les vidéos visionnées avec ton professeur
- Améliore ta prononciation grâce aux entraînements prévus

BBC LEARNING ENGLISH

e for English 5e

A2

Direction pédagogique

Mélanie Herment
Professeur, formatrice
Académie de Paris

Auteurs

Coordination pédagogique
Laura Cursat
Professeur
Académie de Besançon

Virginie Bordat
Professeur
Académie de Dijon

Hélène Chadoeuf
Professeur, formatrice
Académie de Paris

Mélanie Herment

Corinne Létant
Professeur, formatrice
Académie de Paris

Activités TNI
Cindy Mathieu
Professeur
Académie de Versailles

Drama Club
Rupert Morgan

Fluency MC
Jason Levine

didier

Remerciements

Les auteurs et l'éditeur remercient Elisa Gy pour sa relecture critique toujours pertinente et ses précieux conseils.

Ils remercient également tous les collègues formateurs et les enseignants rencontrés pour la richesse de leur réflexion sur la réforme et sur l'enseignement des langues vivantes en général, ainsi que les collègues qui ont accepté de tester avec leurs élèves les chapitres de ce manuel, en particulier ceux du collège Marcel Aymé de Chaussin
et ceux du collège Pierre Alviset de Paris.

Enfin, ils remercient chaleureusement la famille Bryant, Sarah Staunton, Annie Coghlan et Mark Wallace qui ont contribué, par leurs témoignages, à donner au projet son identité culturelle.

Édition : Emily Storey, Claudine Varin
Responsable éditoriale : Catherine Laurent
Conception maquette intérieure : Primo & Primo (Sébastien Jenger);
Isabelle Aubourg (*Great reads for teens*)
Conception couverture : Nicolas Piroux
Mise en page : Isabelle Aubourg (corpus) ; MARSE (*Get better at*)
Illustrations : Johanna Crainmark, Sylvie Eder, Sébastien Jenger, Marc Thomas
Iconographie : Audrey Lamy
Photogravure : RVB photogravure

PAPIER À BASE DE FIBRES CERTIFIÉES

éditions didier s'engagent pour l'environnement en réduisant l'empreinte carbone de leurs livres. Celle de cet exemplaire est de :
1 kg éq. CO_2
Rendez-vous sur www.editionsdidier-durable.fr

 - ISBN: 978-2-278-08752-5

Dépôt légal : 8752/07

Achevé d'imprimer en Italie en avril 2021 par L.E.G.O. (Lavis)

Bienvenue en 5e

Cette année est la première du cycle 4, qui te mènera jusqu'à la fin du collège. L'objectif principal de ce cycle est **l'approfondissement.** Avec *E for English 5e* tu vas pouvoir :

Nouveau cycle, nouveaux défis et nouvelles découvertes !

• Mieux comprendre le monde anglophone moderne en explorant ses origines

Tu as déjà eu un aperçu de **Londres** ? Cette année, tu vas découvrir un événement qui a grandement contribué à la géographie de la capitale britannique...

Tu sais ce qu'est la **Maison Blanche**, et qui y réside ? Tu vas découvrir que le Président n'y est peut-être pas seul...

Tu connais **Harry Potter** ? C'est un héros moderne, certes, mais il a un illustre ancêtre...

• Plonger dans le quotidien de jeunes anglophones

Tu vas découvrir la **littérature de jeunesse** qu'affectionnent les jeunes Britanniques, partager la **vie de jeunes New Yorkais** et réfléchir avec les élèves d'une école américaine à ce que nous réserve l'avenir.

À partir de documents riches et surprenants, tu seras invité(e) à réaliser des tâches motivantes : **organiser une fête d'Halloween, dessiner et présenter une pièce de monnaie commémorative** ou encore **recruter... des pirates** !

• Progresser à ton rythme

Chacun a des **compétences et des stratégies** différentes, aussi avons-nous voulu te donner la possibilité, régulièrement, de choisir les documents qui t'attirent le plus et la manière de les aborder. Tu pourras ainsi réfléchir à la façon dont tu apprends et poursuivre cet entraînement dans les pages *Get better at* et *How to*.

Nous te souhaitons une année heureuse et enrichissante !

Les auteurs

Sommaire

Project 1 That's me!

Project 2 Terror at the White House

CHAPITRE FLASH

The Brilliant World of Tom Gates

À travers son journal intime, découvre un épisode de la vie de Tom Gates.

→ p. 41-44

LANGAGES

Parcours EAC

Documents	Langue	Tâches
Textes • Extraits de *The Brilliant World of Tom Gates*, Liz Pichon **Images** • Dessins de Liz Pichon pour *The Brilliant World of Tom Gates* **Audio** • Flash interview: "Do you like Tom Gates?"	**Grammaire** • Les adverbes **Lexique** • Se préparer pour aller au collège • Mon quartier • Adverbes	**Mini project** Write about your life, Tom Gates-like! ÉVALUATION

Project 3

Save the date!

L'histoire de la Grande-Bretagne... c'est dans la poche ! Sur des pièces ou des timbres, découvre-la en images.

→ p. 45-58

RENCONTRES AVEC D'AUTRES CULTURES

Parcours EAC/CITOYEN

Documents	Langue	Tâches	AP
Textes • BD (imprimée sur des timbres) racontant le grand incendie de Londres **Images** • Timbres et pièces de monnaie commémoratifs • Peinture du grand incendie de Londres **Audios** • Flash interview: "Tell us about the money in your country" • Emeline and Lucinda about British money • The Royal Mint presents its commemorative coins • Samuel Pepys' experience of the Great Fire • Drama Club : *London's Burning!* • Ready for the test?	**Grammaire** • Les pronoms relatifs • Le Présent de narration **Lexique** • L'argent • Repères historiques • Grands personnages • Repères temporels • Le grand incendie de Londres **Prononciation** • Les contractions • Les voyelles « tendues » • L'intonation de phrase	**Entraînement** Create an audio-guide about the new £1 coin Record a radio drama about the Great Fire of London **Tâche finale** Design a coin or a stamp to commemorate British history	**Méthodes** How to make a (great) presentation → p. 51 **Révisions** Ready for the test? ÉVALUATION

TN

Activité numérique
Count your coins!

Have fun with...
Tom Gates and British history

Drama Club
London's Burning!

Sommaire

Project 4 Kids of New York

New York, suivez le guide ! Des adolescents nous font découvrir leur ville : maison, école, amis, activités…

→ p. 59-72

VOYAGES ET MIGRATIONS / RENCONTRES AVEC D'AUTRES CULTURES

TNi
Activité numérique
Spot the place in NYC!
Have fun with… Music
A Day in NYC, Fluency MC
Drama Club
New York, New York, Frank Sinatra

Project 5 Ayy, Matey!

Entre légende et réalité : à la rencontre du monde de la piraterie et des grands pirates anglais ou irlandais qui ont marqué l'histoire et la littérature.

→ p. 73-86

VOYAGES ET MIGRATIONS / RENCONTRES AVEC D'AUTRES CULTURES

EPI **Anglais – Mathématiques**
Chasse au trésor !
→ Programmer un robot pour aller chercher un trésor sur une planète hostile

TNi
Activité numérique
Help the pirate find the treasure!
Have fun with…
Pirate language
Drama Club
Walking The Plank

CHAPITRE FLASH

King Arthur

Du roi Arthur à Harry Potter, qu'est-ce qu'un héros ?

→ p. 87-90

RENCONTRES AVEC D'AUTRES CULTURES

Parcours EAC

Documents	Langue	Tâches
Textes • *Harry Potter and the Chamber of Secrets*, J.K. Rowling (citations) **Images** • Planche de BD : *King Arthur - Excalibur Unsheathed: An English Legend* • Images du film *Harry Potter and the Chamber of Secrets* **Audios** • Flash interview: "If we say 'hero' and 'sword', who do you think of?" • The Legend of King Arthur	**Grammaire** • Le génitif • Le superlatif **Lexique** • Qualités héroïques • Personnages • Temps et lieux	**Mini project** Tell the story of a heroic character ÉVALUATION

EPI **Anglais – Français – Histoire**

Le chevalier, un héros intemporel ?

→ Créer un héros et lui donner vie dans un livre animé

Project 6 Robots

Les robots : quelle utilité dans notre société ? Quel avenir ? Découvre comment les jeunes Américains imaginent le futur !

→ p. 91-104

VOYAGE ET MIGRATION

Parcours AVENIR

Documents	Langue	Tâches	AP
Textes • Article issu du site de l'université d'Elon : *Kids' Predictions for Our Future* **Images** • Quatre robots célèbres • Image du film *Big Hero 6* **Audios** • Flash interview: "What does the word 'robot' evoke for you?" • Annie talks about famous robots • Drama Club: *The Brownie Recipe* • Ready for the test? **Vidéos** • Extrait du film *Big Hero 6* • Vidéo de présentation du concours FIRST	**Grammaire** • Le comparatif • *Will* **Lexique** • Parties du corps • Traits de personnalité • Tâches ménagères • Avantages et risques **Prononciation** • Les interjections • Les sons /əʊ/, /ɒ/ et /ɔː/ • Le comparatif de supériorité	**Entraînement** What robot are you? Write about the future! **Tâche finale** Design a robot and present it to the class!	**Méthodes** How to speak with someone (even a robot!) → p. 97 **Révisions** Ready for the test? ÉVALUATION

TN **Activité numérique**
Robot battle!

Have fun with...
Diary of a Wimpy Kid: Predict your future

Drama Club
The Brownie Recipe

CHAPITRE FLASH

A Native American Tale

Découvre la tradition orale des Indiens d'Amérique. Écoute un conte amérindien, illustre-le et mets-le en scène.

→ p. 105-108

LANGAGES, RENCONTRES AVEC D'AUTRES CULTURES

Parcours EAC

Documents	Langue	Tâches
Images • Photo de Grayhawk Perkins, *storyteller* • Carte géographique : *Native American tribes of Louisiana* • Illustrations *(Native American art)* **Audio** • Flash interview: "What is your favourite tale?" **Vidéos** • Meet Grayhawk Perkins • Grayhawk tells a creation myth: *How The Alligator Got His Skin*	**Grammaire** • Prétérit simple / Prétérit *BE* + *-ing* **Lexique** • Le récit et ses personnages	**Mini project** Tell us a story! ÉVALUATION

EPI **Anglais – Français**
Raconte-moi le monde !
→ Créer et conter un récit des origines

En fin de manuel

EPI → Une mise en œuvre détaillée de toutes nos propositions pour le cycle 4 : www.epi-didier.com

ÉVALUATION → **Dans le guide pédagogique :**
- les évaluations des connaissances
- les évaluations des compétences

Rap in English with Fluency MC

→ Sur le site compagnon : www.didier-eforenglish.com

J'améliore mon anglais en dehors de la classe

J'apprends ma leçon

- Je **me concentre** au calme.
- J'essaie de **me souvenir du cours** et je dis à haute voix les mots ou les phrases dont je me souviens.
- **J'ouvre mon cahier :** je lis, je vérifie que j'ai tout compris, j'apprends phrase par phrase, je mémorise l'ordre des mots, l'orthographe…
- **Je ferme mon cahier** et j'essaie **de restituer ma leçon à l'oral**, puis **à l'écrit.**

Je fais mes exercices

- Je **relis les textes** dans le manuel et je **réécoute les documents sonores** sur le site compagnon. **www.didier-eforenglish.com**
- Si je dois **préparer une petite prise de parole**, je **m'entraîne** en m'enregistrant et en répétant.

Je vais plus loin

- Je regarde des films, des séries ou des émissions en V.O., avec ou sans sous-titres.
- J'écoute parler des personnes :

→ Par exemple sur les sites **www.audio-lingua.eu** ou **www.elllo.org.**

- Je répète et je m'entraîne à bien prononcer :

→ Par exemple sur les sites **www.bbc.co.uk/learningenglish** ou **www.englishcentral.com**

- Je lis de petits articles sur le site de la BBC : **www.bbc.co.uk/newsround**

Quelques conseils pour t'entraîner à l'oral :

Tape ta leçon dans un logiciel de synthèse vocale :

→ Par exemple : **text-to-speech.imtranslator.net**

Cela te permettra d'avoir un modèle oral que tu pourras écouter et répéter.

Enregistre-toi avec un téléphone ou sur un ordinateur :

→ Par exemple : **vocaroo.com**

Puis compare ta performance avec le modèle.

Project
1

That's me!

AUDIO 3

Flash interview:

Can you define yourself in one word?

EPI > Anglais - Arts plastiques :
UN AUTOPORTRAIT EN MOTS ET EN IMAGES

MINI PROJECTS

- Create Mr. Men and Little Misses
- Be the hero of your own story!
- Drama Workshop

FINAL PROJECT

- Create your self-portrait

Skinny, Happy, Funny

Mr. Men and Little Misses

AUDIO 4 Spot the characters

1. **Look!** Can you name some of these characters?
2. **Listen to part 1.** Try to spot the characters!
3. a. Which characters are *not* described?
   b. Can you imagine their names?
4. **Listen to part 2** and discover their identities. Were you right?
5. **Time to write!** Complete a Wall of Fame of Mr. Men and Little Misses. → WB p. 5
6. In groups **Choose a character on p. 12 and describe it to your group.** Who will spot it first?

AP Yes, you can listen to a bit of English p. 18.

Here & there Track 5

	French	English
Male	M.	Mr
Female	Mme	Mrs (married) Miss (single) Ms (don't know)

MINI PROJECT

Create celebrity Mr. Men and Little Misses

→ WB p. 6

- Choose a famous character or a famous person.
- Think about their:

  personality *looks*

- Choose ONE adjective that best describes them: it will be their name!
- Create a card and get ready to introduce your character to the class.

Why not create the class's very own wall of fame with all the cards? ☺

GRAMMAIRE

- Les adjectifs • *Be* et *Have* au Présent simple → WB p. 18-19

TNI Spot the matching symbol

All about me

2 books, 2 heroes, YOUR choice!

1 Look at the book covers and read the first sentence of each text:

BOOK 1

The first thing you should know about me is that...

BOOK 2

There are only ~~six~~ seven things that are important to know about me:

Which text do you want to read?

2 Read the text you have chosen and investigate.

WORK YOUR WAY

a. Make links between the text and the book cover. → WB p. 8

b. What is *not* in the picture? → WB p. 9

c. Complete the book cover or imagine a new one.

Tip

- Concentre-toi **en priorité** sur ce que tu comprends.
- Aide-toi des **illustrations** qui accompagnent ces textes.

BOOK 1

The first thing you should know about
me is that my name is Alvin Ho.
I am afraid of many things.
Elevators.
Tunnels.
Bridges.
Airplanes.
Thunder.
Substitute teachers.
Kimchi.
Wasabi.
The dark.
Heights.
Scary movies.
Scary dreams.
Shots.
School.

Alvin Ho, Allergic to Girls, School and Other Scary Things, Lenor Look, 2009

Yes, you can read a bit of English p. 19.

BOOK 2

There are only ~~six~~ seven things that are important to know about me:

1. I'm 10 years old
2. I live near Wilmington, Delaware.
3. I'm half Irish (red hair!) and half French (I love éclairs!), even though I'm all American.
4. My parents got divorced on November 3.
5. Soccer is my Best Sport. (I play for the Screaming Jonquils.)
6. My best Friend's name is Blanca Hidalgo.
7. My best Heroes are Emily Dickinson, Mother Teresa, Jewel, and Shaquille O'Neal.

Sincerely,

Fiona Claire Jardin

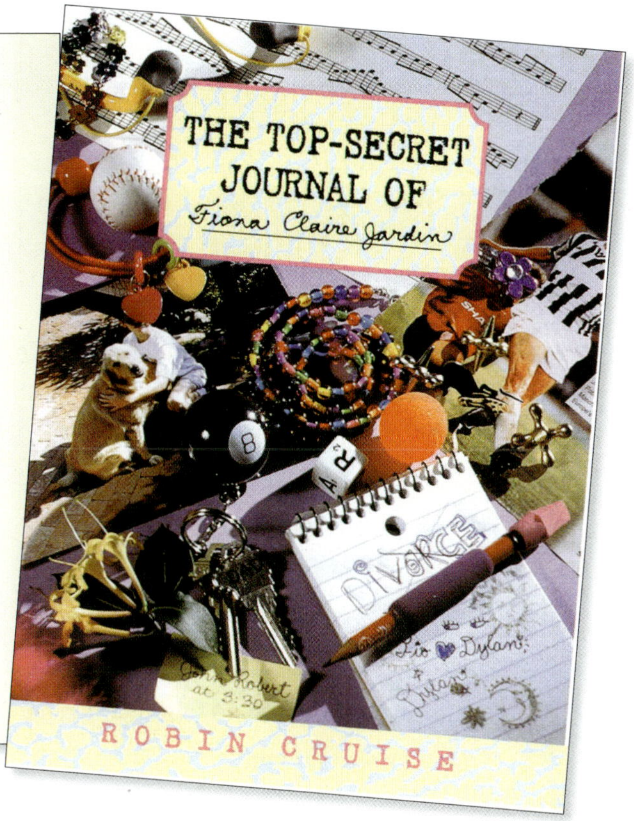

The Top-Secret Journal of Fiona Claire Jardin, Robin Cruise, 2000

3 Time to write!

In groups

WORK YOUR WAY

Imagine a new page from Alvin's book: *"**I am fond of** many things..."*

or

Imagine a new page from Fiona's diary: *"There are **three other things** you should know about me..."*

I Dare you — **Read more extracts from these books on the Internet.**

MINI PROJECT

Be the hero of your own story!

- Choose one of the texts above.
- Adapt it to yourself. → WB p. 10

I Dare you — **Imagine the front cover of your book.**

Tip

- Respecte bien la **forme** du texte d'origine.
- Pour le **contenu**, tu es libre d'imaginer tout ce que tu veux !

GRAMMAIRE

- Le Présent simple • La détermination *(a / an / Ø)* → WB p. 18-19

FRIENDS

"Hey, Charlie"

'I'm Charlie.' I said, not too shy.

'And I'm Patrick. And this is Sam.' He pointed to a very pretty girl next to him. And she waved to me.

'Hey, Charlie.' Sam had a very nice smile.

They both told me to have a seat. [...] They asked me questions.

'How old are you, Charlie?'

'Fifteen.'

'What do you want to do when you grow up?'

'I don't know just yet.'

'What's your favorite band?'

'I think maybe the Smiths because I love their song 'Asleep' but I'm really not sure. [...]'

'What's your favorite movie?'

'I don't know really, they're all the same to me.'

'How about your favorite book?'

'The Side of Paradise by F. Scott Fitzgerald.'

'Why?'

'Because it was the last one I read.'

The Perks of Being a Wallflower, Stephen Chbosky, 1999

Logan Lerman, Ezra Miller and Emma Watson in the movie adaptation of *The Perks of Being a Wallflower* (2012).

Here & there

In this text, "favorite" is spelt the American way. In British English, it is spelt "favourite".
Here are other common differences:

In the US	In the UK
color	colour
theater	theatre
defence	defense
analyze	analyse

1 Read the first lines of the text (1-7).

a. What is the situation?

b. "They asked me questions": what questions do you expect?

WORK YOUR WAY **2 Choose the version of the text that suits you best.**

→ WB p. 11

3 Read the whole text:

a. Can you find the questions you expected?

b. Focus on Charlie's answers. What do they tell you about his personality?

4 Work in pairs.
Pupil 1: You are Charlie and you want to know more about Sam.
Pupil 2: You are Sam. Answer Charlie's questions using the following information:

The Doors | *journalist* | *seventeen* | *Romeo and Juliet* | *Star Wars*

5 Time to write! Here is more information about Charlie.
Use it to continue the dialogue.

English class | *one brother and one sister* | *in an apartment*

→ WB p. 13

Getting to know each other

AUDIO 6 Hey, Emma!

1 Listen to the first seconds of the recording. What do you expect next?

2 Listen to the rest. Were you right?

3 React. Do you share common points with these teenagers?

4 Time to write! Write down the questions and the answers you liked best.

5 In groups Interview each other.

i Dare you Interview... a teacher!

AP Yes, you can speak a bit of English p. 19.

MINI PROJECT

Drama Workshop

In groups

Act out the scene from *The Perks*. You have the choice:

WORK YOUR WAY

- Act out the scene as it is
- or
- Adapt it (to yourselves or to famous people or characters)

GRAMMAIRE

- Les questions en *WH* → WB p. 20
- Les adjectifs possessifs
- Les pronoms personnels

How to... make a good start

Voici quelques astuces pour prendre de bonnes habitudes dès le début de l'année.

Yes, you can listen to a bit of English!

→ Manuel p. 13

Prépare-toi à l'écoute : anticipe !
Tu peux écrire les mots ou informations auxquels tu t'attends afin de les cocher ou de les rayer pendant ou après l'écoute.

Certains mots que tu avais correctement anticipés peuvent t'échapper à l'écoute si leur prononciation n'est pas celle que tu attendais.
ex : *orange*
/'ɒrɪndʒ/

- **Regarde bien la page 12.** Tu vas devoir repérer les personnages mentionnés dans l'enregistrement.
- **À quelles informations ou à quels mots peux-tu t'attendre ?**

Des couleurs ?
blue? green? ...

Des pronoms ?
she? he?

Des adjectifs ?
round? tall? ...

Des vêtements ou accessoires ?
hat? bag?

Sois actif pendant l'écoute : joue au détective !

Pour comprendre le message, prélève des indices :

Les mots accentués
Ce sont les plus importants pour la personne qui parle, et donc ceux sur lesquels elle insiste le plus.
→ « Je prononce » B p. 23

Les mots répétés
S'ils sont répétés, c'est souvent qu'ils sont importants.

L'intonation
Elle peut dire bien des choses de l'intention du locuteur.
Ex : une intonation montante dans une description peut indiquer que cette dernière n'est pas finie...

Yes, you can read a bit of English!

→ Manuel p. 14

Appuie-toi sur les mots que tu connais ou qui ressemblent au français.

Certains mots transparents n'ont pas le même sens en anglais qu'en français (ex : *car*). Fie-toi donc toujours à ton sens logique. ☺

Fais des liens entre le texte et les images.

Fais attention aux indices typographiques (majuscules, ponctuation, gras, italiques...). Ils peuvent t'aider à comprendre la nature d'un mot ou l'importance d'une information.

Établis des liens entre les mots à l'intérieur des phrases.

The first thing **you should know about me is that my name is Alvin Ho.**
I am afraid of many things.
Elevators.
Tunnels.
Bridges.
Airplanes.
Thunder.
Substitute teachers.
Kimchi.
Wasabi.
The dark.

3. I'm half Irish (red hair!) and half French (I love éclairs!), even though I'm all American.
4. My parents got divorced on November 3.
5. Soccer is my Best Sport (I play for the Screaming Jonquils.)
6. My best Friend's name is Blanca Hidalgo.
7. My best Heroes are Emily Dickinson, Mother Teresa, Jewel, and Shaquille O'Neal.

Yes, you can speak a bit of English!

→ Manuel p. 17

Pour bien parler, il faut bien écouter...

- **... les documents proposés.** Ils pourront te servir de modèles. Entraîne-toi à répéter le document « Hey, Emma! » Track 6
- **... ton interlocuteur.** Même si tu t'es préparé(e) à ce qu'on pourrait te demander, peut-être y aura-t-il des surprises ?

Et il faut quelques petites techniques...

- **Demande à ton interlocuteur de répéter ou de reformuler.**
  I'm sorry, can you repeat, please?
  I don't understand... What do you mean?
- **Tu peux, comme Charlie, ne pas savoir quoi répondre... Mais il faut savoir le dire** ☺
  I don't know just yet. *I have no idea right now.*
  Mmm... I don't know, what about you?

Words

All about me

Apprends ces mots avec leur prononciation !

My personality

Track 7

happy = **cheer**ful = **joy**ful /tʃɪə/ ≠ **grum**py

funny

shy ≠ **out**going /ʃaɪ/

clever = **brai**ny = smart

quiet ≠ **tal**kative /ˈtɔːkətɪv/

lazy ≠ **hard**working

helpful

bossy

Hobbies

Track 8

read

sing

listen to **mu**sic

play... an **in**strument / **foot**ball / **vi**deo games

write

watch **mo**vies / TV **se**ries

hang out in the park

surf on the **in**ternet

act

take **pic**tures/ **pho**tographs

Physical description

Track 9

skinny ≠ slim ≠ big

tall

small
short

tiny /aɪ/

HAIR

straight ≠ **cur**ly

brown

short
blond

long
dark

bald /bɔːld/

mous**tache**

beard /bɪəd/

Accessories

Track 10

hat

glasses

scarf (pl. : scarves) /skɑːf/

headband

watch

handbag (GB) = purse /pɜːs/ (US)

Tastes

Track 11

hate

dis**like**/ not like

en**joy**/ like

be fond of / be keen on

love

be a huge fan of / be **cra**zy **a**bout

Learn these words in your workbook

→ WB p. 14-16

→ More exercises in your WB p. 16-17

Je m'entraîne

1 Work in teams. Jouez au « petit Bac » : pour chaque catégorie, trouvez un mot commençant par la lettre que le professeur vous donnera. Quelle équipe sera la plus rapide ?

Personality	*brave*
Action/hobby	*buy*
Clothes/accessory	*b…*
Physical description	…
Colour	…
Celebrity	…

2 Utilise les lettres de ton prénom pour écrire un poème sur toi.

3 Work with a friend.

a. Prépare 5 phrases en utilisant des mots du chapitre… que tu vas effacer.
e. g. *I really like … to music.*

b. Donne ces phrases à ton voisin, qui devra les compléter.

c. Vérifie ses propositions (qui peuvent être correctes, même si elles sont différentes de ce que tu avais prévu !).

4 Choisis un héros (livre, cinéma …), découpe son image et note 5 adjectifs : 3 qui le définissent bien et 2 qui ne lui correspondent pas. Tes camarades devront les identifier !

Matilda

5 À la manière d'Alvin Ho (p. 14), choisis une catégorie ci-dessous et écris la liste correspondante.

What I love | *What I hate* | *Gift ideas*

Je prononce

A Comme un Anglophone Track 12

a. Écoute ces mots. Que remarques-tu à propos de l'accentuation et de l'intonation ?
funny – bossy – helpful – lazy – clever – brainy – happy – cheerful – joyful – grumpy

b. Enregistre-toi et compare.

B Le son /ə/ Track 13

Le fait d'accentuer une syllabe « réduit » les syllabes voisines : on les entend à peine. Beaucoup d'entre elles sont alors prononcées /ə/: clever.
/və/

a. Écoute ces mots : que remarques-tu à propos des lettres soulignées ?
American – quiet – teacher – afraid – moustache – mister

b. Écoute et répète. Es-tu capable d'imiter le modèle le plus fidèlement possible ?

c. Entraîne-toi à bien prononcer.

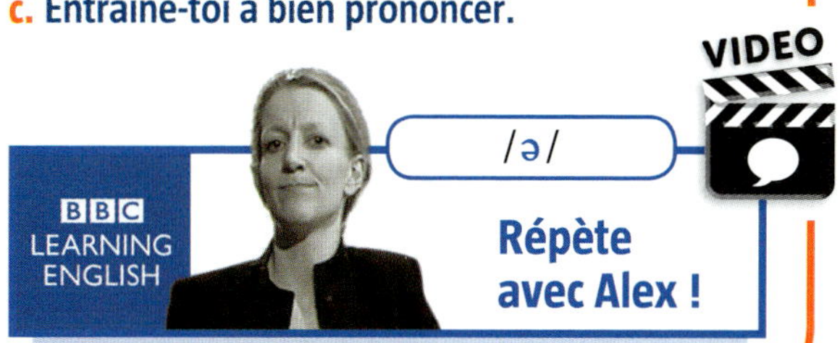

Grammar

→ WB p. 18-21

1 Je veux qualifier quelqu'un ou quelque chose avec un adjectif :

- *She is happy*
- *They are American*
- *He has long legs*

> ! • L'adjectif est INVARIABLE en genre et en nombre.
> • Lorsqu'il est épithète, il se place AVANT le nom qu'il qualifie.

2 Je veux désigner :

- **une personne ou une chose non définie :**

  a boy, a bag, a hat
  an image, an animal

- **des personnes ou des choses non définies ou indénombrables :**

  Ø tunnels, Ø airplanes
  Ø food, Ø love

3 Je veux utiliser le Présent simple :

I	*like*	≠	*don't like*
you	*like*	≠	*don't like*
she/he/it	*likes*	≠	*doesn't like*
we/you/they	*like*	≠	*don't like*

> *I don't = I do not*
> *he doesn't = he does not*

4 Je veux poser des questions à quelqu'un :

WH- + auxiliaire + sujet + (verbe) + (complément) :

- *Why do you like this book?*
- *Where do you live?*
- *What is your favourite book?*

Souviens-toi !

	BE	HAVE
I	*am*	*have*
You	*are*	*have*
He/she/it	*is*	*has*
We/you/they	*are*	*have*

> *you are not / you aren't*
> *he is not / he isn't*

> *I don't have / I haven't got*
> *he doesn't have / he hasn't got*

Pronoms personnels sujets	Pronoms personnels compléments (= pour remplacer un nom)	Adjectifs possessifs (= pour parler des relations d'appartenance)
I	*me*	*my*
You	*you*	*your*
She	*her*	*her*
He	*him*	*his*
It	*it*	*its*
We	*us*	*our*
You	*you*	*your*
They	*them*	*their*

Je m'entraîne

1 Complète logiquement cette mini encyclopédie sur le monde anglophone.

1. Ireland ... an island.
2. The US flag ... blue, white and red. It ... 50 stars and 13 stripes.
3. In Canada, it ... very cold, but people ... used to it!
4. Canberra ... the capital of Australia.
5. In the UK, many people ... tea around 5 p.m.

2 a. Imagine de nouveaux Mr. Men & Little Misses.
b. Décris-les à un camarade qui devra les dessiner !

This character...
These characters...

long tall big	pretty pink/red/ green...	has is have are	hat nose hair...	a an ∅

3 Complète les phrases avec le déterminant qui convient : *a*, *an* ou *∅*.

1. Charlie likes ... rock music.
2. Alvin Ho is crazy about ... superheroes.
3. Fiona Claire Jardin plays ... softball.
4. Sam has two pets: ... cat and ... bird.
5. Charlie has ... older sister, she is ... college student.

4 Les pronoms sont bien pratiques pour éviter les répétitions ! Complète ces phrases avec les pronoms personnels compléments qui conviennent.

1. Fiona Claire Jardin loves Emily Dickinson. Do you know ... ?
2. Alvin Ho is afraid of thunder. Are you scared of ... too?
3. Charlie's favourite writer is Francis Scott Fitzgerald. Do you know ...?
4. Mr Grumpy is always in a bad mood. He can't stand happy people. He hates ....

5 Jeopardy est un jeu américain très célèbre : les candidats lisent des réponses et doivent retrouver les questions qui correspondent. À toi de jouer ! Attention, il peut y avoir plusieurs solutions ☺

Thème : les personnages du chapitre

1. She is half-Irish, half-French... and all American!
2. *The Smiths*.
3. He is allergic to thunder and the dark.
4. He is fifteen.
5. He is blue with white bandages.

Je prononce

A Les liaisons Track 14

Pour que ton anglais semble plus fluide, efforce-toi de faire les liaisons entre les mots.

Écoute et entraîne-toi à répéter les phrases suivantes en faisant bien les liaisons :

1. How old are you, Charlie?
2. They're all the same to me.
3. How about your favourite band?

B L'accent de phrase Track 15

De la même façon que dans un mot, une syllabe est accentuée et pas les autres, dans une **phrase, certains mots sont accentués et d'autres pas.**

a. Écoute et repère les mots accentués :

1. She's blue and round.
2. What do you want to do when you grow up?

b. Classe les mots de ces phrases : comprends-tu pourquoi certains sont accentués et d'autres pas ?

Mots accentués	Mots non accentués

Have fun with...

Self-portraits

FINAL PROJECT

Create your self-portrait. It can be based on the following:

1

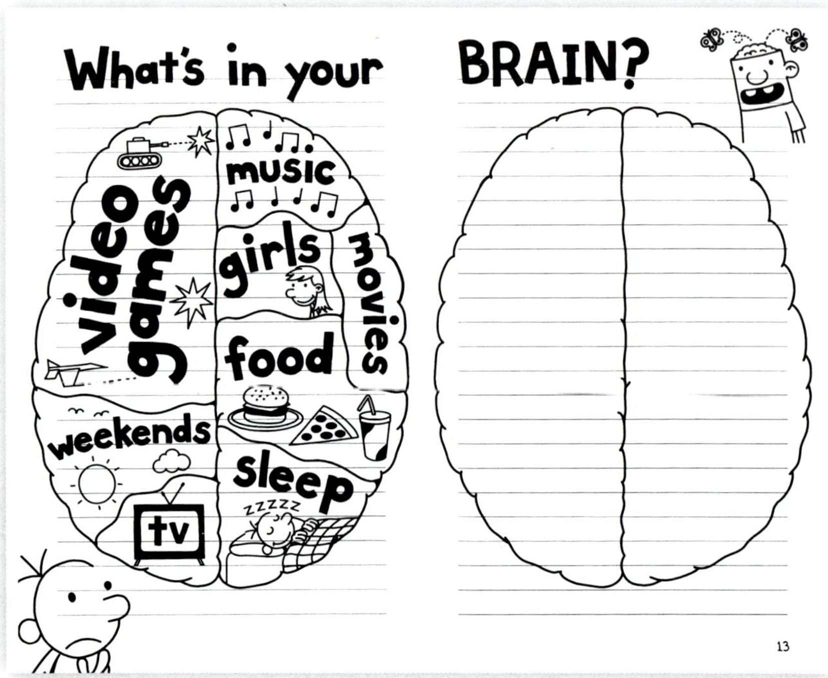

→ WB p. 23

Diary of a Wimpy Kid: Do-It-Yourself, Jeff Kinney, 2011

I Dare you Get to know one of your classmates... and draw their brain!

2

→ MR. MEN AND LITTLE MISS

→ p. 13

3

→ A poem about me

→ p. 21

4

→ All about me

→ p. 15

5

→ A collage about me

→ p. 21

DRAMA CLUB

presents

Meet the Twits

Curtain up.

The CAST, all except Mr and Mrs TWIT, *assemble in a semicircle. Drum roll.*

ACTOR 1:
They're shocking!

ACTOR 2:
They're smelly!

ACTOR 3:
They're silly!

ACTOR 4:
They're stupefyingly stupid!

ACTOR 5:
Get ready to meet...

ACTOR 6:
The one and only...!

ACTOR 7:
Thank goodness!

ALL:
The Twits!

[Fanfare]

[The semicircle splits to admit Mr and Mrs TWIT, *who enter with show-biz flair.*
Mrs TWIT *carries a walking stick. They act out words of the* NARRATORS*]*

ACTOR 8:
The best way to describe the Twits is...

ALL:
Disgusting

[...]

ACTOR 1:
How often you may ask, did Mr Twit wash this bristly, nailbrushy face of his?

ACTOR 2:
The answer is...

ALL:
Never!

MR TWIT:
[Proudly] Not even on Sundays!

ACTOR 3:
As a result there were always hundreds of bits of old breakfasts...

ACTOR 4:
... and lunches...

ACTOR 5:
... and suppers...

ACTOR 6:
sticking to the hairs.

*[*Mr TWIT *licks eagerly round his face]*

ACTOR 7:
Specks of gravy!

ACTOR 8:
Dried-up scrambled egg!

ACTOR 9:
Spinach!

ACTOR 10:
Tomato ketchup!

ACTOR 11:
Fish fingers!

[...]

ACTOR 7:
They're shocking!

ACTOR 8:
They're smelly!

ACTOR 9:
They're silly!

ACTOR 10:
They're stupefyingly stupid!

ACTOR 11:
The one and only...

ACTOR 12:
Thank goodness!

ALL:
THE TWITS!

*[*Mr and Mrs TWIT *take a bow, still fighting]*

[Curtain down]

By Roald Dahl

AUDIO 16

- **Listen to the scene, then rehearse it.**
- **Act out the scene.**

Ready for the test?

ACCOMPAGNEMENT PERSONNALISÉ AP

	Révise	Entraîne-toi
Compréhension de l'oral	**Réécoute** AUDIO 4	**Écoute quelqu'un qui se présente** AUDIO 17 • Exprime comme tu le souhaites tout ce que tu as compris : par des mots ou des phrases / en anglais ou en français / par des dessins / … • Explique-le maintenant par écrit en français.
Expression orale	**Exprime-toi** sur le thème des présentations → Relis **How to make a good start** p. 18-19	**Échange avec un camarade** • Chacun incarne un héros et se présente sans dévoiler son identité. Posez-vous des questions pour découvrir qui est l'autre : âge ? / personnalité ? / apparence ? / … • Comment améliorer vos performances ? donner plus de détails ? / utiliser un vocabulaire plus précis ? / bien accentuer les mots importants ?
Compréhension de l'écrit	**Relis** → les textes p. 14, 15 et 16 → **How to make a good start** p. 18-19	**Lis d'autres histoires sur Alvin Ho et les héros du chapitre** • Feuillette les livres de la série *Alvin Ho* ou *Mr. Men and Little Misses*. • Si tu n'as pas la possibilité de te procurer ces livres en anglais, tu peux taper « Alvin Ho », par exemple, dans la rubrique « Livres » de Google. Cela te permettra d'accéder facilement à des extraits en version originale !
Expression écrite	**Relis** → tes leçons → les **Time to write** dans ton *workbook* → **How to make a good start** p. 18-19	**Deviens auteur à ton tour !** • Écris un texte pour présenter ton héros préféré. • Comment améliorer tes performances ? varier les adjectifs ? / donner plus de détails ? / améliorer l'organisation du texte ? / …

\+ Imagine ce que le professeur pourra te demander dans chaque test

Project 2

Terror at the White House

AUDIO 18

Flash interview:

Can you name three American presidents?

Training Tasks

- Prepare your party planner
- Write a spooky story about the ghost of a former US president

FINAL TASK

- Organize your own Halloween party!

Discover

Halloween at the White House

Be my guest

1. **Look at the document:** what is it? →

2. **Look more closely:** are you allowed to attend this event?

3. **Imagine you are going. Plan the event in your smartphone with the help of our party planner!**

→ WB p. 24

- Use the map below to locate the event.
- Be careful when picking your costume! Look at the recommendations.

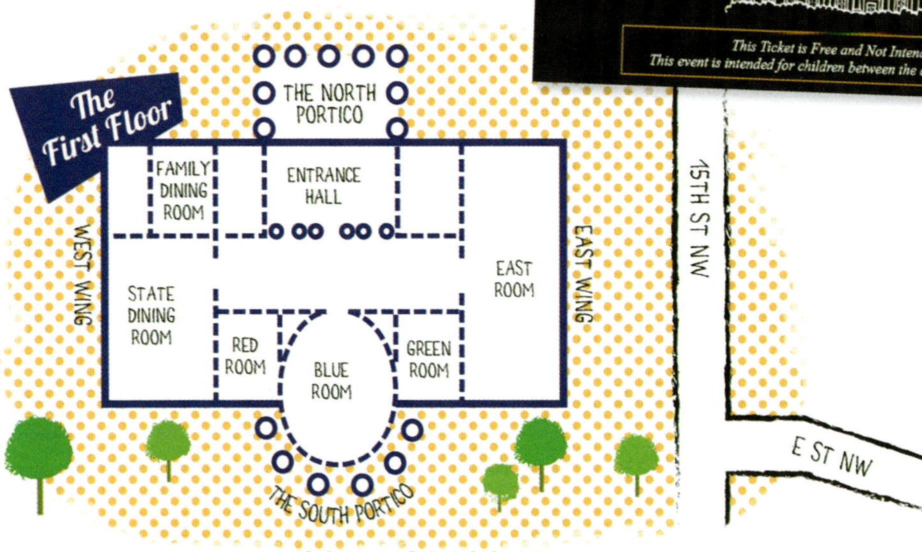

Here & there

The Elysée Palace, Paris	The White House, Washington DC
120,300 sqft*	55,000 sqft*
365 rooms	132 rooms
900 people working there	1,800 people working there
1 level	6 levels
320 clocks	35 bathrooms, 28 fireplaces
President's office	
Le salon doré	The Oval Office

* = square feet *(unité de mesure)*

Enter the White House

VIDEO 1 Trick-or-Treat with the President and First Lady

Obamas dance to 'Thriller' at White House Halloween party

Gregory Korte , USA TODAY Published 8:55 p.m. | Oct. 31, 2016 |

The Obamas decorated the South Lawn of the White House and welcomed more than 4,000 people for trick-or-treating, mostly from 15 Washington-area elementary schools and military families. Treats came in the form of Hershey Kisses, Halloween cookies, M&Ms, Fruit Bars, Kettle Corn, No and Sunny baseball cards and other assorted candies. Tricks were forbidden by the Secret Service.

Obama dressed up as the president of the United States. [...]

Barack Obama (1961-) was the 44th President of the United States. He served two terms of office, from 2009 to 2017.

1. **Read the title of the article and look at the picture.**
   a. What links can you make?
   b. What "tricks" or "treats" do you expect?

2. **Read the article.**
   a. Check your guesses.
   b. Label the treats in your workbook. → WB p. 25

3. "The Obamas decorated the South Lawn of the White House...". Imagine how, then illustrate the map of the White House: what was it like on Halloween? → WB p. 25

4. **Watch the video.**
   a. Who is standing in front of the Obamas?
   b. What new information do you learn about the event?

5. **Time to write!** Use all the information you have to add a new paragraph to the article. → WB p. 26

Training Task

Prepare a party planner for your Halloween party

You are going to organize your own Halloween party!

- **Whole class.** Think about the things you have to plan for your party.
- **On your own.** Fill in your party planner. → WB p. 26
- **Whole class.** Decide on the organisation for D-Day!

GRAMMAIRE

- Dire les nombres et les dates → WB p. 33

Going on a haunted tour

Meet former presidents

VIDEO 2 Haunted White House tour

HALLOWEEN AT THE WHITE HOUSE! (OCTOBER 31, 2016)

The White House tour was such a fun experience. To be in the same place as so much history and beauty is beyond words. To know that all of the presidents have been in the same rooms that I was in for just a moment. One of the Halloween titbits was that Abraham Lincoln foretold his death in a dream and is one of the most famous ghosts to haunt the White House!

George Washington (1732-1799) was the **1st President** of the USA. He led the Continental army in victory over the British during the **American Revolution**. He helped define the role of the president and write the **Constitution**.

Abraham Lincoln (1809-1865) was the **16th president** of the USA. He led the country during the **Civil War**, that opposed the southern states – who wanted their independence and were in favour of slavery – and the northern states. The north won the war and Lincoln issued the **Emancipation Proclamation** which set 4 million slaves free.

heathersspin.blogspot.fr/2016/11/white-house-tour

1. **Are you ready for a haunted tour of the White House?**
   a. Watch the "welcome" video. What can you expect from the tour?
   b. Read the visitor's impressions above. Did she like it?

2. **Look at the pictures.** What is happening?

3. **Read the texts about Lincoln and Washington.** Pick out elements to complete a US presidents timeline. → WB p. 28-29

4. **Time to write! In the video, the tour guide invites you to share your impressions on #hauntedwh.** Use what you have discovered so far to say what you think of this tour.

Do ghosts haunt the White House?

"Footsteps outside the room..."

Lilian Rogers Parks heard footsteps outside the small room where she was working on the second floor of the White House. Then she heard them again. And again. When she looked toward the door, no one was there. How odd; the house was largely deserted. President Franklin Roosevelt, the first lady, and some of the maids were in New York. (Before the advent of air conditioning, first families often left the hot, humid capital for part or all of the summer.)

The room where Parks was working was part of a suite. The adjacent room happened to be home to the Lincoln bed. After an hour, the maid took a break and found another employee on the third floor. "Why do you keep walking across the floor in the Lincoln Room without coming in?" she asked.

That was impossible; he had just come on duty. "That was Abe you heard", he said. Like other workers through the years, he believed President Lincoln's ghost haunted the building.

The White House for kids, A History of a Home, Office and National Symbol, Katherine L. House, 2014

AP How to understand stories p. 33.

1. **Read the title of the text.** What do you expect?

   characters | *events* | *time* | *place*

2. **Now read the text.** Were you right?
3. Work on the text in your workbook. Use the timeline to situate the event. → WB p. 27-29

Tip

Appuie-toi sur :

– les **prépositions** pour repérer les indications de lieux et de temps,

– la présence de **majuscules** pour identifier les noms propres (attention, certains noms communs anglais prennent une majuscule !),

– les **connecteurs logiques** pour comprendre l'enchaînement des événements.

Training Task

Write a spooky story about the ghost of a former US president → WB p. 30

- Choose *the time when the story takes place* | *the former president* | *the room where the ghost appeared*

  (the former president) ↑ Use the timeline → WB p. 28-29

  (the room where the ghost appeared) ↗ Use the map of the White House p. 28

- Write your story.

WORK YOUR WAY: Use the text above **or** write it the way you want.

GRAMMAIRE

- Le Prétérit simple → WB p. 36

TNI Halloween Memory Game

FINAL TASK

Organise your own Halloween party

That spooky Halloween night is getting close, plan your party!

1 Get ready

- **Split the class into 3 groups.** Each group will have one mission.
- **Group 1.** You are in charge of the invitation cards. Think about:

date & time | *place* | *dress code* | *slogan*

- **Group 2.** You are in charge of the programme. Think about:

decorations | *food & drinks* | *Halloween games* | *pumpkin carving*

- **Group 3.** You are in charge of the advertising and decorations. Think about:

Halloween decoration themes | *posters to put up in the school*

☺ **Use your spooky stories to decorate the class.**

2 Have fun!

- On D-Day: get your guests involved in fun activities of all sorts!

I Dare you — **Put out the lights and read your spooky stories out loud...**

How to...

Understand stories *and enjoy them!*

ACCOMPAGNEMENT PERSONNALISÉ

Pour comprendre une histoire, tu n'as pas besoin de connaître le sens de chaque mot : il suffit de quelques stratégies efficaces et de bon sens !

Prépare-toi à la lecture : lis le titre, la première phrase et anticipe la suite du texte.

Fais des liens :
– entre la première phrase et le reste du texte,
– entre les mots à l'intérieur des paragraphes.

Vérifie tes hypothèses.

Repère les majuscules.

Identifie la nature des mots correspondants.

Déduis le sens des mots inconnus grâce au contexte, au champ lexical auquel ils appartiennent ou à leur formation.

"Footsteps outside the room..."

Lilian Rogers Parks heard footsteps outside the small room where she was working on the second floor of the White House. Then she heard them again. And again. When she looked toward the door, no one was there. How odd; the house was largely deserted. President Franklin Roosevelt, the first lady, and some of the maids were in New York. (Before the advent of air conditioning, first families often left the hot, humid capital for part or all of the summer.)

The room where Parks was working was part of a suite. The adjacent room happened to be home to the Lincoln bed. After an hour, the maid took a break and found another employee on the third floor. "Why do you keep walking across the floor in the Lincoln Room without coming in?" she asked.

That was impossible; he had just come on duty. "That was Abe you heard", he said. Like other workers through the years, he believed President Lincoln's ghost haunted the building.

The White House for kids, A History of a Home, Office and National Symbol, Katherine L. House, 2014

Appuie-toi sur :
– les mots que tu connais,
– les mots qui ressemblent au français

Attention, ils n'ont parfois pas le même sens ! Assure-toi que ton hypothèse de sens est logique par rapport à l'ensemble du texte.

À toi de jouer !

1. Continue d'appliquer les conseils ci-dessus à la lecture de ce texte. → WB p. 27
2. Découvre les histoires de fantômes proposées par la Maison Blanche lors du *haunted tour*. → WB p. 125

Words

Halloween

Apprends ces mots avec leur prononciation !

Halloween

Track 19

pumpkin / Jack-O'-**Lan**tern

bat

spider web
/aɪ/

broom

ghost

witch

skeleton
/ə/

haunted house

monster

trick-or-treat

costume

spirit

candy

Spooky stories

Track 20

death *(n.)* / dead *(adj.)*

wicked
/ɪ/

hear

dreadful = **hor**rible

scream

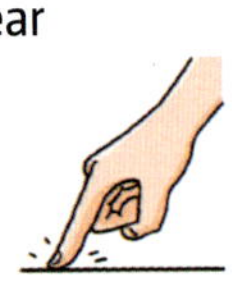
touch

ap**pear**

feel

catch

frightening = **sca**ry

grab

House

Track 21

Party

Track 22

invi**ta**tion *(n.)* / in**vite** *(v.)*
/aɪ/

lo**ca**tion / place

RSVP = please reply to the invitation

join a **par**ty

dress up

give / throw a **par**ty

Learn these words in your workbook

→ WB p. 31-32

Je m'entraîne

1 Work with a friend. *Word or trick!*
Fais deviner un mot à ton camarade (dessin, définition). Compte jusqu'à 10 ; s'il ne l'a pas trouvé, donne-lui un gage qui permette de le mémoriser (épeler le mot en anglais par exemple...).

2 *From basement to attic...* Track 23
Écoute les définitions et identifie les lieux.

3 Regarde attentivement les deux images ci-dessous et trouve les 5 différences.
e.g. *In picture 1 the ..., whereas in picture 2 ...*

1

2

4 Lis ces séries de mots. Chasse l'intrus et trouve un titre à chaque catégorie.
1. cheerful – frightening – dreadful
2. spirit – ghost – wicked
3. costume – gate – room
4. spider – bedroom – bat

5 In groups. *Halloween Bingo!*
Sur une feuille, écris ou illustre 16 mots de la leçon (4 lignes de 4 mots).
Un de tes camarades, muni de son manuel, va annoncer au hasard des mots du chapitre.
Qui aura complété sa grille en premier ?

Je prononce

A Comme un Anglophone ! Track 24

a. Écoute ces noms liés à l'histoire des États-Unis :
Abraham Lincoln – Franklin Roosevelt – George Washington – Barack Obama – The American Revolution – The Constitution

b. Entraîne-toi à les prononcer comme un vrai Anglophone !

B Les sons /θ/ et /ð/ Track 25

a. Écoute les mots suivants :
the – sou**th** – **th**ere – **th**riller – o**th**er – **th**at – **th**row – dea**th** – **th**ree – **th**irteen.

b. Classe-les selon la prononciation de [th].

/θ/	/ð/
...	...

c. Entraîne-toi à bien prononcer.

Grammar

Quand on parle des présidents qui ont résidé à la Maison Blanche, on a besoin du Prétérit pour raconter leur histoire mais aussi de nombres et de dates, pour situer leur époque, par exemple.

1. Je dis les nombres et les dates

Les années

On écrit	On dit
1865	eighteen sixty-five
1809	eighteen-o-nine /əʊ/
1900	nineteen hundred
2017	two thousand and seventeen *OU :* twenty seventeen

Les nombres

On écrit	On dit
132 rooms	one hundred and thirty-two rooms
1,800 people	one thousand eight hundred people
8.95	eight point nine-five

! *hundred* et *thousand* ne prennent pas de -s :
→ deux cents personnes = *two hundred people*
deux mille personnes = *two thousand people*

Les dates

Pour dire les dates on utilise les nombres ordinaux.

On écrit	On dit
Monday 31st October	Monday the thirty-first of October
Monday, October 31st	Monday, October the thirty-first

!

GB	USA
05/11/17	11/05/17
The fifth of November twenty seventeen	November (the) fifth, twenty seventeen

2. Je raconte une histoire au Prétérit simple

1. Lillian Rogers Parks **heard** footsteps outside the small room.
2. When she **looked** toward the door, no one was there.
3. **Did** the employee really **believe** President Lincoln's ghost **haunted** the building?

Pour raconter une histoire au passé ou rapporter des faits révolus, on peut utiliser le **Prétérit simple**.

- À la **forme affirmative** (1, 2), on le construit en ajoutant *-ed* (ou *-d*) à l'**infinitif du verbe**.
- Aux **formes négative** et **interrogative** (3), on utilise l'auxiliaire *did* (Prétérit de *DO*) avec tous les verbes, sauf *BE*.

!
- Certains verbes ont un Prétérit **irrégulier** : il faut l'apprendre par cœur ! (→ voir liste p. 174-175)
- Pour tous les verbes, sauf *BE*, la forme Prétérit est la même à toutes les personnes.

Track 150
Sing, sang, sung
with Fluency MC

→ More exercises in your WB p. 35-39

Je m'entraîne

→ Je dis les nombres et les dates

1 a. Un peu de culture ! Choisis la date qui convient pour chacune des trois phrases ci-dessous et écris-la en toutes lettres.

2/4/1789 9/22/1862 11/4/2008

1. On ..., Barack Obama became the first black president of the USA.
2. George Washington became the first president of the USA on ... .
3. President Lincoln wrote the Emancipation Proclamation on ... .

Tip
Utilise la *timeline* dans ton *Workbook* p. 28-29

b. Peux-tu ajouter une phrase de plus ?

2 Écoute et écris ces dates en toutes lettres. Compare avec ton camarade. Track 26

→ Je raconte au Prétérit simple

3 *Spooktacular story!*
Complète cette histoire avec des verbes de ton choix au Prétérit. Lis-la à tes camarades.

It was the night of Halloween. I ... into my grandma's attic, where I ... a big chest. When I ... it, I ... something touch my shoulder. I ... ! I ... scared. Suddenly, smoke ... . It ... me. I ... to leave quickly but the door was locked!

I Dare you **Écris la fin de cette histoire !**

4 *Are you talking to me?!*
À peine creusée, ta citrouille a commencé à te parler ! Écris la suite de l'histoire.

5 In groups. *Storytelling.*
Chacun à votre tour, ajoutez une phrase contenant un nouvel élément pour continuer l'histoire. Ne vous consultez pas !

character *setting* *problem*

It was the night of Halloween...

Je prononce

A La prononciation de *-ed* Track 28

a. Écoute ces verbes au Prétérit :
looked – happened – asked – haunted – decorated – screamed – helped

b. Classe-les selon la prononciation de la terminaison *-ed*.

/ɪd/	/d/	/t/
...	...	...

c. Que remarques-tu ? Peux-tu trouver d'autres verbes pour chaque catégorie ?

d. Entraîne-toi à les répéter, puis enregistre-toi et compare avec le modèle.

B Les nombres Track 29

Écoute et entraîne-toi à prononcer ces nombres :

30 13 40 14

Fluency MC

Halloween Night

What did you do for Halloween? Did you go out?
No, I stayed in. I watched a horror movie. It scared me out of my skin!
How about you? What did you do? Did you dress up and trick-or-treat?
Did you go to a party? Where did you meet?

On the 31st of October, Halloween night, we threw a crazy party.
We put out all the lights and told spooky stories about witches and ghosts.
There was one about a headless soldier. It was really gross!
We played scary music. We made people scream.
I'm dead serious. We had a blast this Halloween!

We planned the party for months. More than 100 people came.
We served food and drinks and played a bunch of different games.
We had spooktacular fun in an old haunted mansion.
It was filled with spider webs and frightening decorations.
Guests went online to find its secret location.
We all wore scary costumes. It was a wicked celebration!

Did you do anything special for Halloween?
Did you dress up like a gangster, a monster, or a queen?
Did you carve a Jack-O'-Lantern? Did you have a party with your classmates?
What did you do? How did you celebrate?

Lyrics and music by Fluency MC

- **Listen to this song and rap along.**

AUDIO 30

DRAMA CLUB

presents

CHARACTERS

- Darth Vader Kid
- Dracula Kid
- Special Agent 1
- Special Agent 2
- President

Trick or Treat?

DARTH VADER KID:
We've been all over town trick-or-treating! Let's go home now.

DRACULA KID
Wait – what about that big, white house over there? They must be rich...

DARTH VADER KID:
They might give us *tonnes* of candy!

They ring the bell. A Special Agent appears.

DRACULA & DARTH VADER:
SURPRIIISE! TRICK OR-

SPECIAL AGENT 1 *(taking out his pistol)*:
FREEZE! Put DOWN the lightsabre!

DARTH VADER:
...treat?

SPECIAL AGENT 1:
Calling all agents! We have a situation at the East Gate, over!

SPECIAL AGENT 2 *(over radio)*:
Agent Simmons here! I am despatching an intervention force now, Agent Carter! Are you under attack? I repeat – are you under attack, over?

SPECIAL AGENT 1:
Negative! I have two suspicious individuals in custody, over!

SPECIAL AGENT 2:
Agent Carter, are they armed, over?

SPECIAL AGENT 1:
Affirmative. One of them has a lightsabre, sir! Judging by his helmet, he is a Dark Lord of the Sith, over.

DARTH VADER KID:
But I'm not *really*!

SPECIAL AGENT 2:
Carter, can you maintain the hostiles in custody, over?

SPECIAL AGENT 1:
I'm not sure, sir. I believe one of them can transform into a bat, over!

DRACULA KID:
No, I can't!

DARTH VADER KID:
It's true – honestly! He's not really a vampire!

SPECIAL AGENT 1:
Don't try using your Jedi mind tricks on me, Vader! Simmons – where is that back-up?

PRESIDENT:
Right here. It's alright, Agent Carter. I can deal with this.

DRACULA & DARTH VADER:
The... the President???

PRESIDENT:
Trick or Treat! Now, do you want to come inside the White House?

AUDIO 31

- **Listen to the scene, then rehearse it.**
- **Act out the scene.**

☺ You can change the kids' costumes if you want.

Ready for the test?

ACCOMPAGNEMENT PERSONNALISÉ AP

Révise	Entraîne-toi

Compréhension de l'oral

Réécoute

VIDEO 2

Écoute quelqu'un raconter une histoire d'Halloween

AUDIO 32

- Avant l'écoute : à quel type d'informations t'attends-tu ?
- Écoute, puis explique ce que tu as compris, au choix : par des mots ou des phrases / en anglais ou en français / par des dessins / …
- Explique-le maintenant par écrit en français.
- Compare avec un camarade et discutez-en. Quelles stratégies avez-vous utilisées ?

Expression orale

Exprime-toi sur le thème d'Halloween

Échange avec un camarade

- Tu as participé à Halloween à la Maison Blanche : raconte la fête à ton camarade.
- Comment améliorer vos performances ? donner plus de détails ? / utiliser un vocabulaire plus varié ? / bien prononcer la terminaison en *-ed* ? / …

Compréhension de l'écrit

Relis
→ les textes p. 29 à 31
→ How to understand stories p. 33

Visite la page #hauntedwh

- Rends toi aussi sur le site : www.obamawhitehouse.archives.gov/blog/ et consulte l'article « *Inside the Haunted White House* » pour en savoir plus sur Halloween à la Maison Blanche.

Expression écrite

Relis
→ tes leçons
→ les Time to write dans ton *workbook*
→ les Training tasks p. 29 et 31

Rédige une histoire d'horreur pour Halloween

- Partage-la avec la classe. Qui rédigera l'histoire la plus terrifiante ?

+ Imagine ce que le professeur pourra te demander dans chaque test

CHAPITRE
FLASH

Diary

The Brilliant World of Tom Gates

AUDIO 33

Flash interview:

Do you like Tom Gates?

MINI PROJECT

Write about your life, Tom Gates-like!

Discover

A fun way to tell about your life!

Tom Gates's diary – Part 1

Even though I only live four minutes away from my school, I'm often late.

This is usually because me and Derek (my best mate and next-door neighbour) "chat" a bit (OK, a LOT) on the way. Sometimes it's because we get distracted by delicious fruit chews and caramel wafers at the shop. Occasionally, it's because I've had loads of other very important things to do.

1

The Brilliant World of Tom Gates, Liz Pichon, 2001

1 a. Read the first sentence of the text and look at the doodle.
Make links between them in your workbook. → WB p. 40

b. Read the rest of the text and make more links. → WB p. 40

2 Focus on the last sentence. Imagine what these "important things" are.

3 Time to write! Draw a doodle of *your* neighbourhood and write about yourself.

WORK YOUR WAY

You can make your own sentences

or

adapt the text above.

e.g. *Even though I live far away from my school, I am never late...*

Tom Gates's diary – Part 2

For instance, this is what I did this morning (my first day back at school).

Woke up – listened to music
Played my guitar
Rolled out of bed (slowly)
Looked for socks
Looked for clothes
Played some more guitar
Realized I hadn't done my "holiday reading homework"
PANICKED – thought of good excuse for lack of homework (phew!).
Annoyed my sister, Delia. Which I admit did take up a very LARGE chunk of the morning (time well spent though).
Hid Delia's sunglasses.
Took my comic into the bathroom to read (while Delia waited outside – Ha! Ha!).

2

1 Read the text above.

- Make links between the illustrations and the text.
- Draw ✍ more illustrations.
- Tick ✔ the activities you do too in the morning.

→ WB p. 41

2 So what were the "very important things" Tom had to do (question 2 p. 42)?

3 Time to write!

a. Imagine Tom's "good excuse" (l. 12) and write his excuse note for school. → WB p. 42

b. Continue the text: imagine how Tom annoyed his sister (l. 13).

4 React. Do you agree with this review of *Tom Gates*:

> **"Very enjoyable and funny"**
> (*The Guardian*, April 2013)

MINI PROJECT

Write about your life, Tom Gates-like

You too were late for school today! Explain what you did this morning.

Tip
Rends ton récit amusant comme celui de Tom Gates.

GRAMMAIRE
- Les adverbes → WB p. 44

REBRASSAGE
- Le Prétérit simple

Language tools

Apprends ces mots avec leur prononciation !

Words

Getting ready for school

Track 34

wake up

get up / roll out of bed

getting ready:

have **break**fast

take a **show**er

get dressed

look for

do your **home**work

pre**pare**/pack your **school** bag

go to school

be late ≠ be on time

Adverbs

Track 35

When?

- **al**ways
- **of**ten
- **u**sually
- **some**times
- oc**ca**sionally
- **rare**ly
- **ne**ver

How?

slowly ≠ **quick**ly

My neighbourhood

Track 36

bakery
/eɪ/

grocery **store**

close to

far a**way** from

my **next** door **neigh**bour

bus stop

tube sta**tion**
/eɪ/

Grammar

Les adverbes

1. I usually stop by the shop on my way to school.
2. I'm often late.
3. Sometimes it's because we get distracted…
4. Rolled out of bed (*slowly*)

- Pour parler de la fréquence ou de la manière dont on fait les choses, on peut avoir recours à des adverbes.
- Certains adverbes sont composés d'un adjectif auquel on a ajouté *-ly*. Si l'adjectif se termine par un « l », on double ce dernier : *usual* → *usually*

Attention à l'ordre des mots !

En anglais, l'adverbe se place généralement devant le mot sur lequel il porte (un verbe, un adjectif…) :

I usually stop by the shop.

I'm often late.

Exercices

→ WB p. 42-45

Project 3

Save the date!

AUDIO 37

Flash interview:

Tell us about the money in your country

Training Tasks

- Create an audioguide
- Record a radio drama about the Great Fire of London

FINAL TASK

- Commemorate British history!

Discover

British money

This is our money!

AUDIO
38-39
British coins and notes

1 Look at the image.

a. Spot the British currency and its symbol.

b. Guess the value of this note.

2 a. Listen to Emeline talking about British money. Tick the coins mentioned.

Track 38 → WB p. 46

b. Listen again and label the coins with the information you have understood. → WB p. 46

3 Now listen to Lucinda talking about British notes. Label them in your workbook.

Track 39 → WB p. 46-47

4 Time to write!

In groups Design a poster about British money.

Stories to tell

1 Look at the coins on p. 47 closely.

a. What is different from the ones you saw previously?

b. What do these coins have in common? Do you know any of the elements on them?

2 a. Listen and spot these coins as they are mentioned. → WB p. 47

b. Listen again and circle the elements mentioned, then label the coins.

3 In groups Design a timeline and place the events portrayed on the coins.

Complete your timeline all along this chapter.

4 Time to write! Each coin has its "own story to tell".

In groups Choose one of the coins and complete its story. → WB p. 48

AUDIO 40

The Royal Mint presents its commemorative coins

The Royal Mint is an agency that produces coins for Britain.

1

2

3

4

Training Task

Create an audioguide about the new £1 coin.

You are working for the Royal Mint. Tell the story behind this coin.

- Read a short text by the Royal Mint and use it to label the coin. → WB p. 48
- Record your audioguide and prepare to share it with the class.

e.g. *This coin has a leek, which is the symbol of...*

Tip

Réécoute les documents audio de ces pages et relève des expressions qui pourront t'être utiles pour réaliser ton audioguide.

AP How to make a presentation p. 51.

GRAMMAIRE

- Les pronoms relatifs → WB p. 57

REBRASSAGE

- Dire les nombres et les dates
- Le Prétérit

TN Count your coins!

Understand

History... with stamps!

"At about 4 in the morning..."

AUDIO
41-42
Saturday Drama: Samuel Pepys' experience of the Great Fire

BBC RADIO The Great Fire of London LISTEN

Radio dramas are a great British tradition. The BBC produces hundreds of radio plays each year.

1 **Look at the picture and read the information:** what do you expect?

place | *characters* | *situation* | *moment*

2 a. **Listen to part 1.** Track 41
What do you learn about the situation?
What do the noises indicate?
b. **Listen to part 2.** Track 42
How does the situation evolve?

3 **Prepare your training task! Listen again and:**
a. Draw a sketch of the different settings.
b. Complete the lines of the characters in your workbook. → WB p. 49

4 **Time to write!** Write Samuel Pepys' diary of that day.

In the heat of the action

1 **Look at the documents on p. 49:** what are they?

2 **Read them and compare with the radio drama.**
a. What more do you learn here?
b. Use the streets mentioned to locate the fire on Google Earth.

3 **"The fire spreads rapidly":** see how rapidly in your workbook. → WB p. 51

4 **Time to write!** Choose one stamp and imagine the corresponding dialogue for the BBC radio drama. → WB p. 52

Complete your timeline.

Training Task

Record a radio drama about the Great Fire of London

WORK YOUR WAY

Use the script from the BBC drama → WB p. 49 **or** the dialogue you have created → Time to write! p. 48

- Cast the characters: *storyteller* | *Samuel Pepys and his wife* | *his maid* | *Thomas Farriner and his daughter* | ...
- Rehearse your scene and record your radio drama! **Don't forget the sound effects ☺**

GRAMMAIRE

- Le présent de narration → WB p. 59

FINAL TASK

Let's commemorate!

Design a coin or a stamp to commemorate a major event in the history of Britain.

Jane Austen, c. 1790

1 Get ready

1665	The Great Plague of London	The Great Plague strikes London. Thousands of people flee the capital.
1707	The Act of Union	THE KINGDOM BECOMES UNITED!
1807	The Slave Trade Act	ENOUGH WITH SLAVERY!
1815	The Battle of Waterloo	WELLINGTON VS NAPOLEON. THE FINAL BATTLE.
1817	Jane Austen dies	Major British writer Jane Austen dies, leaving Elizabeth Bennett and Darcy orphaned.
1865	*Alice in Wonderland* is published	GET READY TO DREAM... AND BEWARE THE QUEEN OF HEARTS!
1870	Charles Dickens die	*Beloved Charles Dickens, father of David Copperfield, dies in his home of Gad's Hill Place.*
1997	*Harry Potter and the Philosopher's Stone* is published	THE MOST IMAGINATIVE DEBUT SINCE ROALD DAHL!

Tu es intéressé(e) par **un autre événement ou un autre écrivain** ? Demande des conseils à ton professeur pour faire des recherches à son propos.

- **Choose the event you want to work on.** Learn about it with documents given by your teacher.
- **Choose how you want to commemorate it (a coin or a stamp?).** Prepare your notes accordingly.

name of the event | *date* | *summary of what happened* | *notable facts* | *commentary on the coin or stamp*

2 Action!

- **Design your coin or your stamp.**
- **Present it, using your notes.**

Tip

Pense à **scanner ta réalisation** et à la donner à ton professeur. Cela permettra de la projeter le jour de la présentation : tes camarades la verront mieux ☺.

How to...

Make a great presentation

ACCOMPAGNEMENT PERSONNALISÉ AP

Quand on présente un sujet, il faut être clair et explicite, et savoir captiver son auditoire !

Introduis le sujet.

- **Choisis un des audios des pages 46 et 47** Tracks 38-39-40
  - → Prête attention à la manière dont le narrateur introduit son sujet et chaque partie de l'exposé.
  - → Relève les expressions employées, tu pourras les réutiliser pour ta propre présentation.
  - → Fais attention à l'intonation et à l'accentuation.

Sois explicite !

- **Réécoute la présentation des pièces** Track 38
  - → Que fait Émeline pour s'assurer que les auditeurs vont bien comprendre ? ☺ Elle utilise cette stratégie de 0'30 à 0'39 par exemple.
  - → Prête attention au choix des mots, à l'accentuation et à l'intonation.

Articule clairement les différentes parties de ta présentation.

- **Réécoute les audios présentant les pièces** Track 38 **et les billets** Track 39.
  - → Comment les personnes qui parlent passent-elles d'un objet à l'autre ?
  - → Relève les expressions employées, tu pourras les réutiliser pour ta propre présentation.
  - → Fais attention à l'intonation et à l'accentuation.

Donne des détails permettant à l'auditeur de visualiser ce dont tu parles.

- **Choisis un des audios de la page 46** Tracks 38-39
  - → Prête attention aux détails donnés pour permettre de visualiser et à la manière dont ces détails sont introduits.
  - → Échange avec un camarade qui a travaillé sur un autre audio et mettez en commun vos découvertes.
- **Réécoute la présentation des pièces par la *Royal Mint*** Track 40
  - → Comment le narrateur fait-il pour nous faire découvrir ces événements historiques « comme si on y était » ?

À toi de jouer !

1. Choisis un extrait d'un des audios des pages 46-47 et entraîne-toi à le répéter aussi fidèlement que possible.
2. Les Britanniques n'ont pas l'euro ! Choisis une pièce ou un billet et enregistre un court audio pour le leur présenter.

Words

Apprends ces mots avec leur prononciation !

A country's heritage

Money
Track 43

a coin /kɔɪn/ / a note (UK) = a bill (US)

a **pen**ny / two pence

a pound / the pound

a purse /pɜːs/
a **wal**let

change

price

spend

buy /baɪ/

Memorable people
Track 44

famous

great / **me**morable /ˈmemrəbəl/

1812 1870

be born / live ≠ die
/lɪv/ /daɪ/

Time
Track 46

- be**fore** ≠ **af**ter
- **dur**ing
- for *(+ durée)*
- at 3 in the **mor**ning
- at a**bout** 4 in the after**noon**
- in *+ mois ou année*
- on *+ jour ou date*

Historical landmarks
Track 45

e**vent**

commemo**ra**tion *(n)* / com**me**morate *(v)* / **ce**lebrate

anni**ver**sary /ænɪˈvɜːsərɪ/

des**cribe** / tell = nar**rate**

history

a **sto**ry

Learn these words in your workbook

→ WB p. 54-55

The Great Fire of London
Track 47

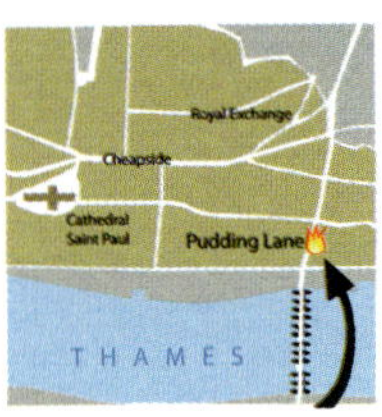

start = **break** out

spread

burn /bɜːn/ / des**troy** = **ra**vage /ˈrævɪdʒ/

es**cape** = flee

→ More exercises in your WB p. 55-56

Je m'entraîne

1 Écoute Lucinda donner davantage d'informations sur une personne célèbre figurant sur un billet. Retrouve le billet et légende-le avec plus d'informations.
Track 48 → WB p. 46-47

2 Écoute maintenant Lucinda parler de 2 personnes importantes pour l'histoire du Royaume Uni : laquelle devrait à ton avis figurer sur un billet ? Imagine ce billet et dessine-le. Track 49

3 À l'aéroport de Londres, tu es arrêté(e) par un agent des douanes qui vérifie le contenu de ton bagage à main et te pose quelques questions.

– What's in your bag?
– I have my passport, my ..., and some ... .
– Do you have a lot of money with you?
– No, no just a few ... and three twenty pound ... .
– What are you here for?
– I'm going to my friends' to ... Guy Fawkes Day. I'm a student in ..., you see and so I'm very much interested in discovering how you ... this ... .
– Alright then, have a nice stay!

4 Choisis la bonne préposition dans chaque phrase :

1. The event happened *in/on* July.
2. My appointment at the doctor's is *in/on* Monday.
3. Emily was born *in/on* Wednesday, October 6th.
4. Ethan was born *in/on* September 17th.

5 Complète cette biographie de Churchill et enrichis-la avec les adjectifs qui conviennent.

Winston Churchill was born ... November 30, 1874 and died ... January 24, 1965. He became Prime Minister ... May 10, 1940, that's to say ... the Second World War and only one year ... the beginning of the Second World War. First, he was in office ... 5 years. Then he was elected again ... 1951 ... 1955. He was a ... politician who was also ... for his sense of humour.

Je prononce

A Comme un Anglophone ! Track 51

a. Écoute les contractions suivantes :
tuppence – cuppa – whatcha – gimme – kinda – wanna – gonna

b. Écoute-les à présent dans des phrases. Comprends-tu de quelles expressions elles sont les contractions informelles ?

c. Entraîne-toi à les répéter, puis enregistre-toi et compare avec le modèle.

B Les voyelles « tendues » Track 52

a. Écoute deux séries de mots et compare la prononciation des lettres en gras.

- p**ur**se – b**ur**n – b**or**n – st**or**y – anniv**er**sary – g**ir**l
- c**u**t – b**u**t – n**o**t – m**o**ney – s**u**nny

Que remarques-tu ? Classe-les dans ce tableau :

/ɜː/	/ʌ/	/ɔː/	/ɒ/
...	...	...	...

b. Entraîne-toi à bien prononcer ces mots.

Grammar

Quand on veut raconter un événement et donner à ceux qui nous écoutent l'impression « d'y être », on peut utiliser le Présent simple. On a souvent besoin des pronoms relatifs pour donner des précisions et développer notre récit.

1. Je donne des précisions à l'aide de pronoms relatifs

1. This note has our most famous prime minister **who led** us through the war: Winston Churchill.
2. We have a ten-pound note, **which is** a yellowy orange.
3. It commemorates the event **that changed** the landscape of our capital.
4. These are the coins Ø people **use** everyday.

Pour relier deux propositions, on peut utiliser des **pronoms relatifs**. Il faut faire attention à leur fonction dans la phrase, ainsi qu'à leur antécédent pour les employer correctement :

	Fonction : sujet du verbe de la relative	**Fonction :** complément d'objet du verbe
antécédent non animé	which, that	which, that, Ø
antécédent animé	who, that	who(m), that, Ø

Pour trouver facilement la **fonction du pronom relatif**, cache-le et regarde le verbe de la subordonnée relative : a-t-il un sujet ? Si oui, le pronom est complément, si non, c'est lui le sujet ! ☺

2. J'utilise le Présent simple pour raconter une histoire

1. In 1666, a blaze **began** in a bakery, that **raged** through the city for five days.
2. Fire **breaks out** in a bakery on Pudding Lane. Thomas Fariner and his daughter **escape** through a window.

- Pour rapporter des événements qui ont eu lieu dans le passé, on peut utiliser le Prétérit (1) mais aussi, comme en français, le **Présent** (2). Ce dernier permet **d'ancrer le récit dans une réalité plus forte, on a l'impression d'y être !**

- Le Présent simple est particulièrement approprié pour rapporter une succession d'événements, comme c'est le cas dans les timbres p. 49. On s'en sert aussi souvent à l'oral pour rapporter une anecdote.

Rappels :
- Il se contruit à partir de la forme infinitive du verbe.
- On ajoute un *-s* à la 3e personne du singulier *(break**s**)*.
- On utilise l'auxiliaire *do* pour former des phrases interrogatives et négatives (sauf quand le verbe est *be*).

Track 150
***Sing, sang, sung* with Fluency MC**

→ More exercises in your WB p. 58-62

Je m'entraîne

→ Les pronoms relatifs

1 Complète ces devinettes dont le sujet est Londres, puis trouve ce dont il est question.

1. It is the **place** ... the Queen lives.

2. It is a **statue** ... is in Trafalgar Square.

3. He is the **man** ... will be Queen Elizabeth II's successor on the throne.

4. She was the first **monarch** ... was both Queen and Empress of India.

5. It is the **place** ... all the British monarchs are crowned.

6. It is a **means of transport** ... is common in London. It is red.

2 Complète cet article sur les célébrations qui ont eu lieu en 2016 à Stratford-upon-Avon pour commémorer la mort du grand dramaturge William Shakespeare.

Hundreds of people, ... came from all over the country, attended Shakespeare's Birthday Parade on the morning of Saturday 23rd. All the places in ... Shakespeare lived were offering a wild range of interesting activities. The activity ... I liked the most consisted in trying Stage fighting techniques. The actors ... usually perform Shakespeare's plays gave the visitors swords so that we could fight! The swords ... we used were fake but it was fun!

→ Le Présent de narration

3 Découvre Guillaume le Conquérant de l'autre côté de la Manche !

a. Rappelle le contexte dans lequel la bataille de Hastings est survenue (conjugue les verbes au Prétérit).

Edward the Confessor, who ... *(be)* the King of England, ... *(die)* in 1066. As Britain ... *(need)* a new king, Harold II ... *(become)* the king. But William the Conqueror, who ... *(live)* in Normandy, ... (think) he ... *(deserve)* the throne himself, so he ... *(decide)* to invade Britain because, hey, that's how it ... *(happen)* then!

b. Raconte maintenant la bataille à partir des notes que tu trouveras dans ton *workbook*. Tu peux la raconter au Présent afin de transporter le lecteur au cœur de l'action !

Sept. 27, 1666 William the Conqueror
→ set sail from Normandy with 700 ships
and 15,000 men.

→ WB p. 61

Je prononce

L'intonation de phrase Track 53

a. Réécoute cette phrase tirée du *radio drama* p. 48 en faisant attention à l'intonation.

The 2nd of September, 1666. Lord's Day. At about 3 in the morning, our maid, Jane, does come to our chamber door...

b. Recopie-la dans ton cahier et indique à l'aide de flèches (□ et □) quand l'intonation monte et quand elle descend.

c. Observe ensuite la ponctuation de la transcription ci-contre : que remarques-tu ?

d. Écoute à nouveau l'échange entre Mr Pepys, sa femme et Jane et indique l'intonation sur le script dans ton *workbook*. Track 41 → WB p. 49

Have fun with...

Tom Gates and British history!

"Kids' Tapestry" by Liz Pichon marks Battle of Hastings anniversary

English Heritage - 1 August 2016

An all-new version of the Bayeux Tapestry created by Tom Gates writer and illustrator Liz Pichon is unveiled, featuring key historic moments from the past 950 years.

The first panel shows William the Conqueror defeating Harold at the Battle of Hastings in 1066, which inspired the original Bayeux Tapestry.

Panel three shows the Black Death plague arriving in England in 1346.

www.english-heritage.org.uk/learn/1066-and-the-norman-conquest/the-kids-tapestry/

I Dare you Make your own tapestry about an event from British history.

DRAMA CLUB

presents

CHARACTERS
- Mr Pepys
- Will, his servant
- Lieutenant
- Boatman

London's Burning!

Mr Pepys and his servant, Will, go out to look the fire.

WILL:
It looks mighty fierce, don't it, Mr Pepys, Sir?

MR PEPYS:
Yes, Will, it does.

WILL:
Will it spread, Sir? What if it crosses all of London Bridge, and all those homes on it? Where are you going Mr Pepys?

MR PEPYS:
Down to the bridge.

WILL:
Do you think that's wise Mr Pepys?

MR PEPYS:
Come along!

And on our way down, we did meet the lieutenant of the Tower.

LIEUTENANT:
Mr Pepys?

MR PEPYS:
Huh?

LIEUTENANT:
Mr Pepys, is that you, sir? One of my officers said it began at the King's bakery, Mr Pepys, in Pudding Lane.

MR PEPYS:
A bakery?

LIEUTENANT:
Yes, Mr Pepys. And now it's burned St Magnus Church and most of Fish street, and is upon Thames Street.

MR PEPYS:
Come on, Will, we must find a boatman.

WILL:
Yes, Mr Pepys.

* * *

BOATMAN:
You want *me* to go under the bridge?

WILL:
Yes.

BOATMAN:
I don't want my boat set alight.

WILL:
Neither do we.

MR PEPYS:
The fire isn't *on* the bridge.

BOATMAN:
It will be in a jiffy*, though, won't it? You can see it on the end there.

WILL:
We can find another boatman if you won't take us.

MR PEPYS:
We'll pay you double.

BOATMAN:
Under the bridge it is!

* in a minute (informal)

BBC Radio 4, Saturday Drama

AUDIO 54

- **Listen to the scene then rehearse it.**
- **Find the adequate costumes and props and act out the scene ☺**

Ready for the test?

ACCOMPAGNEMENT AP PERSONNALISÉ

Révise	Entraîne-toi

Compréhension de l'oral

Réécoute AUDIO 40

→ Relis **Yes you can listen to real English** p. 18.

Écoute Annie parler d'une pièce AUDIO 55

- Anticipe à partir du titre : à quoi peux-tu t'attendre ?
- Écoute le document plusieurs fois, en essayant de ne pas interrompre la lecture.
- Explique ce que tu as compris :
  par des mots ou des phrases | par des dessins | en anglais ou en français | ...

→ Découvre des détails croustillants de l'histoire britannique en tapant « BBC Horrible History » dans un moteur de recherche.

Expression orale

Exprime-toi sur la monnaie britannique

→ Réécoute les pistes 38 et 39 et essaie d'imiter les personnes qui parlent.

→ Relis la page **How to make a presentation** p. 51.

Présente une pièce à un camarade

- Choisis une des pièces du chapitre et présente-la à un(e) camarade.
- Comment améliorer tes performances ?
  être plus méthodique ? | améliorer l'intonation des phrases ? | mieux réaliser les sons /ɜː/ et /ɔː/ ? | ...

Compréhension de l'écrit

Relis

→ la bande dessinée p. 49

Un nouveau fait historique !

- Rends-toi sur le site *Project Britain*, rubrique « history ». Choisis un fait historique et relève quelques dates et événements.
- Ajoute-les à la frise chronologique que tu as créée au cours du chapitre.

Expression écrite

Relis

→ tes leçons et les **Time to write**

Légende la tapisserie

- Prépare un petit texte pour accompagner l'illustration conçue pour la Peste Noire (p. 56).
- Utilise ces notes pour rédiger ton texte (pense bien aux conjugaisons) :

– in London
– start : in Asia – travelled to England because of black rats on the ships

– no cure – very contagious
– killed 50 million people in Europe (= 60% of the population)

+ Imagine ce que le professeur pourra te demander dans chaque test

Project 4

Kids of New York

AUDIO 56

Flash interview:

What does "New York City" evoke for you?

Training Tasks

- An extra day in NYC!
- The Broadway Dreamer

FINAL TASK

- Shoot a video clip about your life in NY

or

- Write a report about Kids of France

New York City

Take a tour with Jack and Finn

VIDEO 3 A day in New York City

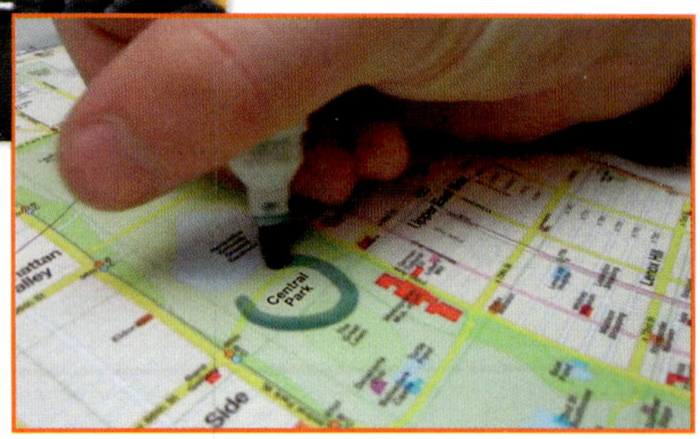

1. **Look at the pictures.**
   a. What do you expect?
   b. Do you know the spot circled on the map? → Can you name other places in New York City?
2. **Watch the first part of the video.** Were you right?
3. a. **Now watch the whole video.** Which places did you recognize?
   b. **Trace** Jack and Finn's itinerary on a map of New York City. → WB p. 63
4. **Time to write!** Label the pictures of New York City. → WB p. 64

At home Discover more places around the world with Jack and Finn's YouTube channel.

"I love it here!"

1. **Look at the poster on p. 61.** Can you spot some elements from Jack and Finn's video?
2. **Read the comments** next to the document. Match each of them with an element from the poster. → WB p. 66
3. **Time to write!** Add your comments about two other elements in the poster. → WB p. 66
4. **Do these things "make you love New York"?** What do you prefer about this city?

TNI Spot the place in NYC!

Having a PICNIC in Central Park

SAYING THE STATUE of LIBERTY looks bigger in the movies

Hearing the tapping of MAHJONG TILES ON WOODEN BOARDS IN CHINA TOWN

Eating pizza like a NEW-YORKER: fold it over and eat it with your fingers

Singing along WITH THE STARS of BROADWAY

Here & there

The Statue of Liberty

Designed by French sculptor Frédéric August Bartholdi, it was a gift to the United States from the people of France to celebrate the 100 years of the Declaration of Independence in 1886. It is situated in Manhattan on Liberty Island, NYC.

There is a Statue of Liberty in France.
Do you know where it is?

Training Task

An extra day in NYC!

In groups

Jack and Finn are spending a second day in New York.
Play their roles as they are walking around the city and admiring new spots. Think about:

monuments | *places of interest* | *activities* | ...

→ WB p. 67

GRAMMAIRE
- Le Présent *BE* + *-ing*

→ WB p. 74

REBRASSAGE
- Les noms en *-ing*

Understand

Kids of New York

In love with NYC

VIDEO 4 "A place that I've fallen in love with"

1. **Watch part 1.** What part of New York does it show? How do you know?

2. **Watch part 2.**
   a. Were you right?
   b. Focus on the lights and sounds. What can you say about the atmosphere?

3. **Watch part 3.**
   a. What were Julian's feelings when he first discovered this place? What about now?
   b. Julian compares New York City with his hometown. How about *your* hometown and New York City?

4. **Time to write!** Answer this question asked on a forum:

Browse forums ▾ All | New York forums | New York City forum

Search

What's the best one word to describe NYC? ❤ Save Topic
Mar 16, 2006, 1:20 PM

busy? **dynamic?** **exciting?** **over-the-top?** **noisy?** **magnetic?**

Kids of New York

1. **Look at the pictures and titles on p. 63.** What do you expect?

WORK YOUR WAY

2. Choose **text 1** or **text 2** and discover a New York kid.
   a. **Read the text that you have chosen.** What do you learn about the kid's daily life? → WB p. 68
   b. Do you understand the choice of her nickname?

3. Get ready to introduce the kid you have discovered to the class.

Tip

Tu peux te concentrer sur la 1re **phrase de chaque paragraphe**, elle t'aidera à savoir ce qui va être développé ensuite.

Text 1

The Backpacker

Layah Jones, 12, Canarsie, Brooklyn

This is what's in Layah Jones's neon-rainbow backpack with butterfly wings: day planner, language arts binder, math notebook, Spanish and math and drama and work and study skills folders, copy of "The Giver" by Lois Lowry, Rubik's cube, wallet, combination lock, plastic pouch of pens and pencils and stapler and white-out and highlighters.

This is what's in her rubber swim bag: swimsuit, towel, swim cap, goggles, flip-flops. This is what's crammed into her little pink lunch bag to sustain her for a day that starts at 7 a.m. and ends after 8 p.m.: red grapes, Twinkie, potato chips, chocolate pudding, Jell-O with fruit, zipper bag of Lucky Charms, snack mix. [...]

Layah is getting a ride to school from her mother, but after school she has to take a shuttle bus and then a one-hour city bus ride to swim practice near her home. These are the logistics of life in New York, where parents (and kids) go the extra mile — many extra miles — to find a good school.

The Theater Nerd

Text 2

Dorothy Maskara, 12, Sunnyside, Queens

Dorothy Maskara of Sunnyside, Queens, was 3 when she saw the Broadway musical "Legally Blonde" for the first time. "When the curtains go up, I was like, Oh, my gosh, it's like a whole house on the stage!"

Dorothy saw the show nine more times.

At age 12, she has seen 40 or 50 shows (it helps when your mother worked for a company that designs theater merchandise, as hers did).

It is a Wednesday afternoon. Dorothy pauses on her way to singing lessons in the theater district and offers a whirlwind tour* of some of her favorite spots.

She walks among the crowds as dazzled as a first-timer. "I love Times Square because it's so loud, and I'm really loud," she yells. "I can relate to Times Square."

* *une visite éclair*

New York Times, "What Makes a New York City Kid?" by Andy Newman Oct. 21, 2016

Training Task

The Broadway Dreamer

In the manner of *The New York Times* article above, write a short article about Julian. Video 4

Don't forget to include the following information:

name | *age* | *hometown* | *place of residence* | *hobbies* | *dreams* | ...

AP How to organize a text p. 65.

GRAMMAIRE

- Les déterminants → WB p. 77

REBRASSAGE

- Le Présent simple

FINAL TASK

My life in NYC

Take part in The New York Times *project. Imagine you live in New York. Shoot a video to make French people discover your city!*

In 2016, *The New York Times* asked young New-Yorkers to talk about their city.

1 Get ready

- **Choose your nickname:**

  The Early riser — The Observer
  The Adventurer — The Jogger
  ...

- **Imagine your life in NYC:** →

- **Prepare what you are going to say.**
  → WB p. 69

Tip

- Regarde à nouveau les vidéos et inspire t'en. **Videos 3 et 4**
- Pour les images, exploite tout ce qui dans ton environnement peut évoquer New York !
  – le square du coin pour Central Park
  – de célèbres enseignes américaines
  – ...

- **Rehearse the different scenes before shooting your video.**

2 Shoot your video clip

or

Kids of France!

The New York Times *now wants to do a special report about "Kids of France".*

- Contribute by writing a short text about:

  the place where you live | *your everyday life*

- Publish it on a collective Padlet wall along with a picture of your choice.

How to…
Organize a text *effectively!*

ACCOMPAGNEMENT AP PERSONNALISÉ

Un bon récit doit susciter l'attention du lecteur dès les premières lignes.
Pour cela, deux éléments essentiels : bien construire son texte et donner des détails.

Construis ton récit autour d'une idée forte que tu suivras tout du long.

Commence par une anecdote frappante.

Indique clairement la chronologie.

N'hésite pas à ajouter des détails intéressants ou des citations pour rendre ton récit plus vivant.

Quelle est l'idée forte et le fil conducteur de ce texte ?

The Theater Nerd

Dorothy Maskara, 12, Sunnyside, Queens

Dorothy Maskara of Sunnyside, Queens, was 3 when she saw the Broadway musical "Legally Blonde" for the first time. "When the curtains go up, I was like, Oh, my gosh, it's like a whole house on the stage!"

Dorothy saw the show nine more times.

At age 12, she has seen 40 or 50 shows (it helps when your mother worked for a company that designs theater merchandise, as hers did).

It is a Wednesday afternoon. Dorothy pauses on her way to singing lessons in the theater district and offers a whirlwind tour of some of her favorite spots.

She walks among the crowds as dazzled as a first-timer. "I love Times Square because it's so loud, and I'm really loud," she yells. "I can relate to Times Square."

New York Times, "What Makes a New York City Kid?"
by Andy Newman Oct. 21, 2016

À toi de jouer !

1. Applique les mêmes stratégies de lecture au texte 1 p. 63 afin de comprendre comment il est écrit.
2. À ton tour, rédige un court récit. → WB p. 128

Words

New York

Apprends ces mots avec leur prononciation !

A city

Track 57

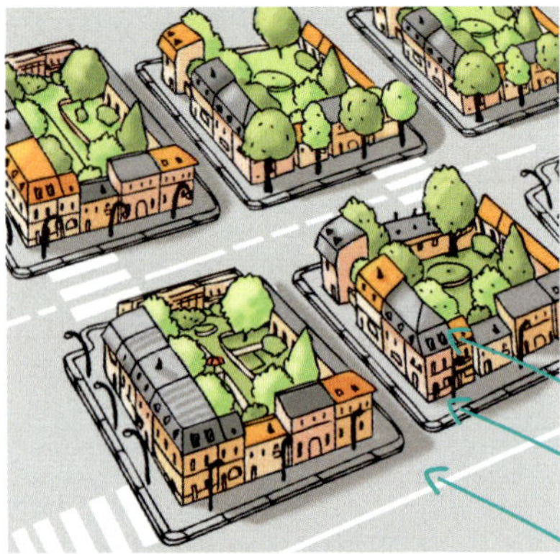

district / **bo**rough /rəʊ/

river

bridge

park

station

church /ca**the**dral /kəˈθiːdrəl/

downtown

statue

Places of interest

Track 58

monument

zoo

ice rink

visit / hit a spot

musical /ˈmjuːzɪkəl/

theatre /ˈθɪətə/

show

sight /saɪt/

spot

Means of transport

Track 59

the **sub**way

subway **sta**tion

ticket

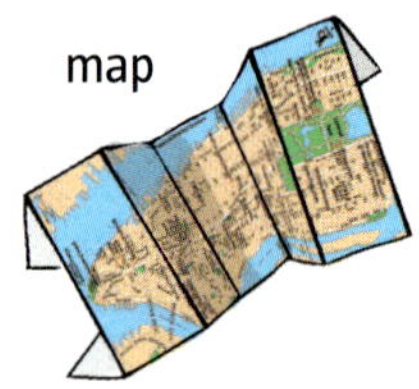

map

ferry

bus / **shut**tle bus /ˈʃʌtl/

cab

Travelling

Track 60

work out / plan a trip

get a ride

travel to

tour

start from

Learn these words in your workbook

→ WB p. 70-71

→ More exercises in your WB p. 72-73

Je m'entraîne

1 Voici des lieux célèbres de New York. Retrouve le mot manquant dans chaque pancarte.

building – park – square – river – avenue – bridge

Empire State ...	Brooklyn ...	Times ...
Fifth ...	Hudson ...	Central ...

2 Work in pairs. Pense à un mot du chapitre. Donne la première lettre de ce mot à un camarade qui devra épeler le mot entier.

3 La communication téléphonique est très mauvaise. Essaie de deviner ce que ton correspondant a voulu dire.

Hi! You know what? I went to New York last week to see a ... in Broadway. I bought myself a ... card to travel in the subway – it was very convenient. I also took a ... to go and see the Statue of Liberty. Loved it! After that, I went to see the Brooklyn ..., which connects Manhattan and Brooklyn. It was great to ... all those places!

4 *Competition time!* En groupes, regardez cette image pendant une minute. Quel groupe réussira à nommer le plus d'éléments ?

5 Work with the class. Un mot et un mime !

- **Chacun de vous choisit un mot p. 66 et l'écrit sur un morceau de papier.**
- **Pioche un mot et fais-le deviner à la classe en ne donnant qu'un indice.**

Ex. : Tu as pioché bridge

tu dis Brooklyn

→ Si personne ne trouve, tu peux essayer de mimer le mot !

Je prononce

A Comme un Anglophone ! Track 61

a. Écoute ces mots enregistrés avec l'accent britannique puis avec l'accent américain. Entends-tu la différence ?

theater – center – river – ferry – ice rink – tour

b. Entraîne-toi à les répéter en prenant successivement les deux accents.

B Les sons /æ/, /ɑː/ et /eɪ/ Track 62

a. Écoute les mots suivants :

start – plan – cab – map – station – park – sidewalk – avenue – skyscraper

b. Classe-les selon la prononciation du [a] : Attention, il y a un intrus !

/æ/	/ɑː/	/eɪ/
...	...	...

c. Entraîne-toi à les prononcer.

Grammar

Quand on veut faire découvrir une ville, des lieux ou monuments particuliers à d'autres personnes, on a besoin du Présent* BE + -ing *pour donner des explications, et de déterminants pour désigner ces lieux.

1. J'utilise le Présent *Be + -ing*

We did the Empire State Building, now we're jumping into a cab to the High Line.

BE conjugué au présent — Infinitif du V + *-ing*

• Pour apporter **des explications**, pour faire « plus » que seulement informer, on peut utiliser le **Présent** ***BE*** + ***-ing***.

Ici, Jack ne nous informe pas du fait qu'il prend un taxi (on le voit bien), il explique **pourquoi** il le prend : pour se rendre à la High Line. Il emploie donc le **Présent** ***BE*** + ***-ing***.

• **Pour poser une question,** il suffit de placer l'**auxiliaire** ***BE*** devant le sujet.

Orthographe :

• Quand le verbe se termine par un « e », ce dernier disparaît :
come → coming

• Quand le verbe comporte une seule syllabe et se termine par « consonne-voyelle-consonne », on double la dernière consonne :
stop → stopping

2. Les déterminants

Construction et emploi

• **Je veux designer une personne ou une chose non définie,** j'utilise « *a* » lorsque le mot qui suit commence par un son consonne et « *an* » lorsqu'il commence par un son voyelle.

→ *a* ***district*** / *a* ***musical*** / *a* ***bus*** → *an* ***avenue***

• **Je veux parler d'une généralité, sans précision,** j'utilise « *Ø* ».

→ *Ø Skyscrapers are very high buildings.*

• **Je veux parler de quelque chose de défini, je considère que la personne à laquelle je m'adresse connaît l'objet ou la personne dont je parle :** j'utilise « *the* ».
« *The* » introduit des noms au singulier et au pluriel.

→ *The statue in front of you is the Statue of Liberty*

THE BIG APPLE

→ More exercises in your WB p. 74-79

Je m'entraîne

→ Le Présent *Be + -ing*

1 Tu es un reporter. Présente New York aux téléspectateurs.

> New York is incredible. Right now, I … *(walk)* down 7th Avenue to reach Times Square. And I can tell you, Times Square is very crowded. People … *(take)* photographs with famous characters in costumes. Others … *(dance)*: I think they are tourists. I suppose they are delighted to be here in this very mythic place. Someone … *(sing)* Frank Sinatra's song *New York, New York*. He is an excellent singer, I have to admit. Further down, I … *(approach)* a couple who … *(take)* a selfie with the Father Duffy* monument behind them. The atmosphere is fantastic!

* *famous American soldier, priest and military chaplain*

2 Amy, une jeune Londonienne, est partie à New York avec sa sœur. Écoute l'audio de leur video blog et dessine ce qu'elles font à New York. Track 63

→ Les déterminants

3 Regarde ces photos. Peux-tu dire ce dont il s'agit ? Légende chacune d'entre elles en faisant attention aux déterminants.

1

2

3

4

5

4 Le *New York Times* va publier un article sur le zoo de Central Park à New York mais le rédacteur a quelques doutes au sujet des articles. Aide-le à les corriger.

> … Central Park zoo is located near … southeast corner of … Central Park. There are … sea lions, … red pandas, … grizzly bear and many other animals. … tickets are very expensive but if you are … child under 2, it is free! There is … 4-D theater in … zoo and … children generally love it!

Je prononce

A L'auxiliaire *BE* conjugué au présent Track 64

a. Écoute des phrases et pour chaque forme réduite de *BE*, trouve sa forme pleine.

b. Répète ces phrases. Enregistre-toi et compare. Es-tu satisfait ?

B La terminaison *-ing* Track 65

a. Écoute les phrases suivantes.

1. We're heading to the Empire State Building.
2. We're jumping into a cab.
3. We're skateboarding in New York.

b. Que remarques-tu à propos de la terminaison *-ing* ? Et de l'accentuation des verbes ?

Have fun with...

Fluency MC

A Day in NYC

New York City: It's Brooklyn and Queens, the Bronx,
Staten Island and Manhattan in between. The Big Apple.
Gotham. The City that never sleeps. Come with me
on a journey through its avenues and streets.

We're spending the day in New York City.
Climbing to the top of the Statue of Liberty, taking the ferry
back to Manhattan. We're downtown, walking around.
There's so much happening! Let's buy MetroCards and take
the subway. Let's go to midtown to catch a Broadway play.

New York City: It's Brooklyn and Queens, the Bronx,
Staten Island and Manhattan in between. The Big Apple.
Gotham. The City that never sleeps. Stick with me
on a journey through its avenues and streets.

Let's check out the lights and colors in Times Square.
It's noisy but it's thrilling. There are people everywhere!
It's lunchtime. We're in Central Park, grabbing a bite.
Now let's jump in a cab so we can see more sights.
We'll have just enough time to visit the Met before we
head to the Brooklyn Bridge and cross the river at sunset.

New York City: It's Brooklyn and Queens, the Bronx,
Staten Island and Manhattan in between.
New York is crowded, dynamic, sometimes over-the-top.
Exciting or overwhelming, the action's non-stop.

Lyrics and music by Fluency MC

AUDIO 66

- Listen to this song and rap along.

DRAMA CLUB

presents

New York, New York

Start spreading the news, I'm leaving today
I want to be a part of it, New York, New York
These vagabond shoes, are longing to stray
Right through the very heart of it, New York, New York

I want to wake up in a city, that doesn't sleep
And find I'm king of the hill, top of the heap

These little town blues, are melting away
I'm gonna make a brand new start of it, in old New York
If I can make it there, I'll make it anywhere
It's up to you, New York, New York

New York, New York
I want to wake up in a city, that never sleeps
To find I'm a number one, head of the list,
Cream of the crop at the top of the heap

These little town blues, are melting away
I'm gonna make a brand new start of it, in old New York
If I can make it there, I'm gonna make it anywhere
It's up to you, New York, New York

By Fred Ebb

AUDIO 67

- Listen to this song.
- Sing along!

Ready for the test?

ACCOMPAGNEMENT PERSONNALISÉ AP

	Révise	Entraîne-toi
Compréhension de l'oral	**Réécoute** Videos 3-4	**Écoute quelqu'un parler de Central Park** (AUDIO 68) • Explique ce que tu as compris, au choix : par des mots ou des phrases / en anglais ou en français / par des dessins / ... • Explique-le maintenant par écrit en français. • Compare avec un camarade et discutez-en.
Expression orale	**Exprime-toi** sur le thème de NYC → Question 4 p. 60 → Enregistre-toi et écoute. Es-tu satisfait(e) ?	**Échange avec un camarade** • Énoncez les monuments et lieux que vous avez envie de visiter à New York.
Compréhension de l'écrit	**Relis** → les textes p. 63	**Apprends-en plus sur New York** • Visite le site : www.nycgo.com • Consulte certaines rubriques comme ***Things to Do*** puis ***Events***. • Tu peux aussi explorer le reste du site, il y a plein de choses à y découvrir !
Expression écrite	**Relis** → How to organize a text p. 65	**Crée un poster avec un plan de New York** • Conçois des petits textes et des illustrations pour commenter ce qui t'intéresse ou t'étonne le plus : lieux, monuments, restaurants... • Comment améliorer ta production : donner plus de détails ? / situer un lieu plus précisément ? / penser aux majuscules ? / faire attention aux articles ? / ...

\+ Imagine ce que le professeur pourra te demander dans chaque test

Project

5

Ayy, Matey!

AUDIO 69

Flash interview:
What do you know about pirates?

EPI > Anglais-Maths : CHASSE AU TRÉSOR !

Training Tasks

- Create an infographic about pirates
- Apply to a pirate league

FINAL TASK

- Create a form to recruit new pirates!

The world of piracy

The word "pirate" comes from the Greek word "peirates", which means "attacker".

Q When did pirates exist?

A There were pirates a long time ago, even in Ancient Rome. But the Golden Age of piracy was in the 17th century, after the discovery of the New World (America) in 1492. The pirates wanted the wealth transported from these far away countries.

Q Who were the most famous British and Irish pirates?

Edward Teach, a.k.a. Blackbeard
Sir Francis Drake
Jack Rackham, a.k.a. Calico Jack
Anne Bonny
Henry Every a.k.a. Long Ben

Q Why did pirates wear eye patches?

A When you move from daylight to darkness, your eyes need a long time to adjust. When pirates went below deck, the eye with the patch adjusted to the dark more quickly.

Q What did pirates eat?

A Pirates often fell sick because they did not eat good food. They often had their teeth falling out and their skin going pale!

Q Why did pirates wear earrings?

A Pirates wore earrings because they believed earrings helped to improve their eyesight. It was also a tradition for young pirates to wear earrings to celebrate their first crossing of the Equator.

Long John Silver
Probably the most famous pirate who never was! Long John Silver is one of the main characters in *Treasure Island*. No pirate inspired more myth and legend than him.

Q Why do pirates have parrots as pets?
A Pirates often appear in films with pet parrots on their shoulders. But this image is purely fictional: it was created by Robert Louis Stevenson in his book *Treasure Island* (1883).

Treasure Island

This book tells of an adventure to an island in the West Indies, where the treasure of a great pirate is buried. This story generated many pirate myths... like using an X to mark the spot on a treasure map, and exotic tropical islands.

Q Do pirates still exist?
A Yes, there are still pirates around today, especially in the Caribbean and Far East (essentially terrorists who attack ships at sea). There are also computer pirates (or hackers).

Fun facts

1. **Read only the questions.** Try to guess the answers!
2. **Now, read the answers.** Were you right? → WB p. 81
3. **In groups** **Quiz time!**
   a. Memorize as much as you can from the infographic.
   b. Prepare 5 questions for the other groups.
   c. Battle time! Close your books and quiz the other teams. Who wins?
4. **Time to write!** Write your own Q&A about piracy. → WB p. 82

Training Task

Audioguide — AUDIO 70

Create a new infographic about pirates

In groups

- Discover more information about pirates: listen to an audioguide and select what seems important.
- Prepare an infographic. Don't forget to illustrate it!

→ WB p. 83

GRAMMAIRE
- Les questions en *WH-* → WB p. 90

REBRASSAGE
- Le Prétérit

Imagine

You are a pirate!

THE VERY NEARLY HONORABLE LEAGUE OF PIRATES

Servin' the High Seas for 152 Years

MEMBERSHIP APPLICATION

How to fill in a form p. 79.

Name: Hilary Westfield

Desired piratical nickname: The Steadfast Scoundrel

Age: 13

Home port: Queensport Harbor

Talents (check all that apply):

[✓] knot-tying [✓] sailing [ ] swordsmanship

[✓] chantey singing [ ] parrot maintenance

[ ] mapmaking [✓] digging [ ] cannon-firing

[ ] magic use [✓] shouting [✓] swimming

[✓] ruthlessness

Can you tread water?* [✓] yes, for 37 minutes [ ] no

Are you allergic to parrots? [ ] yes [✓] no

* float in water by moving your legs

Name three items a pirate must never be without:

a cutlass, a fancy hat, and a fearsome reputation

List three places suitable for hiding a treasure:

a desert island, a hollow tree, and an abandoned shipwreck

Who is your favorite pirate from history or literature?

Long John Silver

Why do you want to become a pirate?

I simply can't imagine doing anything else.

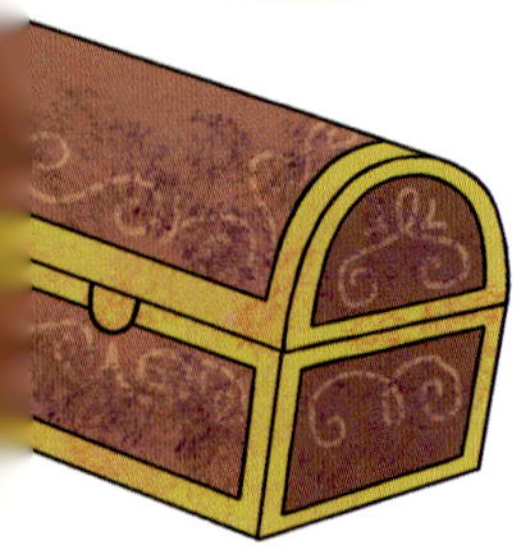

Thank you for your application!

The VNHLP looks forward to seeing you soon on the High Seas.

Magic Marks the Spot (The Very Nearly Honorable League of Pirates #1),
Caroline Carlson, 2013

Becoming a pirate

1 **Look at the document and read its title.**
What do you think a "membership application" is?

2 **Now read the document.**

a. Who asked the questions? Who answered them?

b. Work on the text in your workbook. → WB p. 84

Tip

Ce document comporte beaucoup de **noms composés**. Utilise l'aide dans ton *workbook* pour les comprendre.

3 In groups **Discuss Hilary's application.**
You are the League of Pirates: do you want to hire her?

4 **Discover the pirates' response** in your workbook: do they agree with you?
→ WB p. 85

5 **Time to write!**
Complete the pirates' letter. → WB p. 86

AUDIO 71 Treasure map

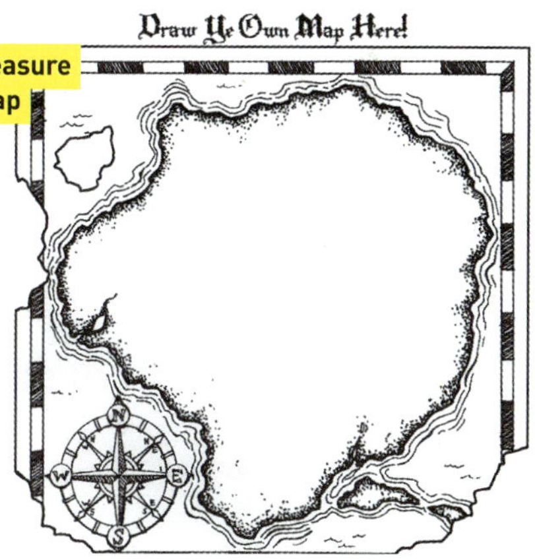

Treasure hunt

1 **Hilary has found a treasure map in a bottle!**
Listen to her describing it and draw the map. → WB p. 86

2 **Compare with your classmates:** are your maps similar?

Training Task

Apply to the League

Submit your own application form to the League. → WB p. 87

I Dare you **Send it to the author... and try to get published!**
http://carolinecarlsonbooks.com/

GRAMMAIRE

- Les noms composés → WB p. 93

TNI Help the pirate find the treasure!

FINAL TASK

Recruit new Pirates!

You are now part of the crew! It's your turn to hire new pirates for the League. Create a new form for the candidates.

1 Get ready

- **Choose the kind of pirate you need and think about their function:**

  a parrot keeper | *a doctor* | *a cook* | ...

- **Remember the basic elements in a form.**

  name | ... | **+ Think about new categories!**

Tip
Inspire-toi du formulaire p. 76 de ton manuel.

- Think about the type of questions you can ask:

  open questions | *mutiple choice questions* | *sentences to fill in* | ...

2 Action!

- **Prepare your questions and get the form ready.**
- **Submit the form to your classmates.**
  Who will you take on board?

☺ Hire 3 pirates and give them their certificates!

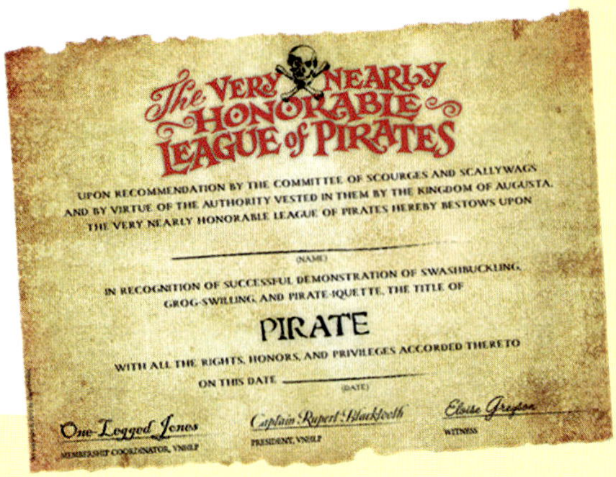
The Very Nearly Honorable League of Pirates

UPON RECOMMENDATION BY THE COMMITTEE OF SCOURGES AND SCALLYWAGS AND BY VIRTUE OF THE AUTHORITY VESTED IN THEM BY THE KINGDOM OF AUGUSTA, THE VERY NEARLY HONORABLE LEAGUE OF PIRATES HEREBY BESTOWS UPON

(NAME)

IN RECOGNITION OF SUCCESSFUL DEMONSTRATION OF SWASHBUCKLING, GROG-SWILLING, AND PIRATE-IQUETTE, THE TITLE OF

PIRATE

WITH ALL THE RIGHTS, HONORS, AND PRIVILEGES ACCORDED THERETO

ON THIS DATE
(DATE)

One-Legged Jones — MEMBERSHIP COORDINATOR, VNHLP
Captain Rupert Blacktooth — PRESIDENT, VNHLP
Eloise Greyson — WITNESS

How to... fill in a form successfully!

ACCOMPAGNEMENT PERSONNALISÉ

Pour remplir correctement un formulaire, il faut bien le comprendre et savoir à quoi il sert... même si c'est pour devenir un pirate !

Qui a établi le formulaire ?

À quoi sert le formulaire ? À quoi t'engages-tu quand tu le remplis ?

Quelles informations te demande-t-on ?

Comment te demande-t-on de répondre ?

THE VERY NEARLY HONORABLE LEAGUE OF PIRATES

Servin' the High Seas for 152 Years

MEMBERSHIP APPLICATION

Name: Hilary Westfield

Desired piratical nickname: The Steadfast Scoundrel

Age: 13

Home port: Queensport Harbor

Talents (check all that apply):

[✓] knot-tying [✓] sailing [ ] swordsmanship
[✓] chantey singing [ ] parrot maintenance
[ ] mapmaking [✓] digging [ ] cannon-firing
[ ] magic use [✓] shouting [✓] swimming
[✓] ruthlessness

Can you tread water? [✓] yes, for 37 minutes [ ] no

Are you allergic to parrots? [ ] yes [✓] no

Name three items a pirate must never be without:

a cutlass, a fancy hat, and a fearsome reputation

List three places suitable for hiding a treasure:

a desert island, a hollow tree, and an abandoned shipwreck

À toi de jouer !

1. Découvre d'autres formulaires et remplis-les attentivement. → WB p. 130
2. À ton tour, établis un formulaire original pour recruter de nouveaux membres dans ta ligue :

The Very Nearly Honorable League of... Vampires | Wizards | Sportsmen | Detectives | ...

Soumets-le à tes camarades !

Words

Adventure

Apprends ces mots avec leur prononciation !

At sea

Track 72

ship

shipwreck

crew /uː/

Travel

Track 73

sail

ex**plore**,
look for / search

travel /
go on a trip

dis**co**ver

Pirates

Track 74

at**tack**

capture

rob

scary / /eə/
menacing /
ruthless /ruːθ/

bury a **trea**sure /e/ /eʒ/

Prepositions of place

Track 75

in the **mid**dle of — a**bove** — **next** to — be**tween** /iː/ — in

on / on top of — be**hind** — through /ð/ — down — up

Places

Track 76

Learn these words in your workbook

→ WB p. 88-89

→ More exercises in your WB p. 89-90

Je m'entraîne

1 In groups. **Walk the plank!** Sur le mode du jeu du pendu, fais deviner des mots du chapitre à tes camarades en les faisant... marcher sur la planche. À chaque lettre erronée, ils feront un pas de plus !

2 Le célèbre Barbe-Noire est recherché... mais rares sont ceux qui l'ont vu de près. Écoute la description d'une jeune recrue et dessine son portrait-robot. Track 77

3 Des intrus ont eu l'audace de se cacher dans les listes de mots suivants. Jette-les par-dessus bord et remplace-les par des mots qui conviennent.

1. shipwreck – plank – sea – deck
2. travel – spot – explore – discover
3. treasure map – gold – jewels – money chest
4. North – West – Down – East

4 Peux-tu indiquer au capitaine où il a égaré ses affaires ?

5 Repère les pirates sur la carte. Chacun veut se rendre dans un endroit précis. Écoute les indications de l'équipage et trouve leurs destinations. Track 78

Je prononce

A Comme un Anglophone ! Track 79

pirates – treasure – menacing – money – ocean – explore – biscuits – capture

Ces mots sont proches de mots français. Pourtant, leur prononciation est bien différente.

a. Comment les prononcerais-tu ?

b. Écoute et vérifie.

c. Entraîne-toi à bien les prononcer.

B Les sons /eɪ/ et /aɪ/ Track 80

a. Écoute ces mots en faisant attention à la prononciation des lettres soulignées.

island – pirate – sail – eye patch – nickname

b. Classe-les selon la prononciation des voyelles soulignées :

/eɪ/	/aɪ/
...	...

c. Entraîne-toi à bien prononcer.

Grammar

Qui étaient les pirates ? Ont-ils vraiment existé ? Autant de questions que ces personnages fascinants soulèvent. Leurs surnoms, des noms composés très évocateurs, ont contribué au mythe.

1. Je pose des questions ouvertes

Avec *DO*	Avec *BE*
❶ When did pirates exist? ❷ Why do pirates have parrots as pets? ❸ What did pirates eat?	❹ Who was Long John Silver? ❺ Where are the modern pirates?

Le noyau de toute question est : auxiliaire + sujet + verbe.

On peut y ajouter des mots interrogatifs.

L'auxiliaire doit être **conjugué** : par exemple au Présent simple (❷, ❺) ou au Prétérit simple (❶, ❸, ❹).

Avec le verbe *BE* :
- il n'y a pas besoin d'auxiliaire en plus, *BE* joue lui-même ce rôle.
- *BE* s'accorde avec le sujet qui suit.

Pour te souvenir de cela, pense à la question ***How are you?*** que tu connais bien !

Principaux pronoms interrogatifs	Ils permettent notamment d'interroger sur :
what	la nature de quelque chose
where	un lieu, une destination ou une origine
when	un moment dans le temps
why	la raison de quelque chose
who	l'identité de quelqu'un
how	la façon dont on fait quelque chose, ou encore l'humeur de quelqu'un, son âge...

2. J'assemble des noms

❶ Pirates usually wore eye patches and peg legs. They used treasure maps to explore desert islands and find treasures!

❷ Some of the most famous British pirates are Blackbeard, Calico Jack and Long Ben.

En anglais, comme en français, on peut créer des noms à partir de divers assemblages. Par exemple :

nom + nom   adjectif + nom   verbe + nom *(swimming pool)*

Je m'entraîne

→ Je pose des questions

1 Work with a friend

a. Tu rencontres le capitaine Jack Sparrow. Pense à 3 questions que tu pourrais lui poser.

b. Joue la scène avec un camarade qui, lui, imaginera les réponses.

2 Cette lettre, écrite par un jeune pirate, a pris l'eau.

Ahoy mum!
Four weeks since we left Plymouth. On the boat, we wore eye patches because .
Yesterday, we finally arrived .
The crew treasure in the sand.
is probably the bravest pirate in the world and we all admire him!
Fair Winds to ye ☺

a. Pose les questions permettant d'obtenir les informations manquantes.

b. Essaie de trouver les réponses à ces questions.

3 Un(e) de tes camarades a été recruté(e) par la Ligue des Pirates. À son retour au collège, tu as plein de questions à lui poser !

What ... ? Where ... ?
How ... ? Who ... ?
Why ... ? How long ... ?

Tip
Besoin de vocabulaire? Utilise un dictionnaire ou ton lexique p. 155.

→ J'assemble des noms

4 Tu connais beaucoup de noms composés.

a. **Trouve ceux correspondant à ces définitions :**

1. The place you go when you want to swim.
2. The person who drives the bus.
3. The keys to open the door.
4. The rooms you study in at school.
5. The jewels on your ears.
6. The exercises you do at home.
7. A restaurant where you eat quickly.

b. **En connais-tu d'autres ? Fabriques-en au moins trois à partir des éléments ci-dessous et prépare des définitions que tu soumettras à tes camarades.**

police •	• box
bed •	• room
ear •	• table
boy •	• man
dining •	• ring
mail •	• friend
note •	• book

5 Work in teams. Défiez l'équipe adverse en leur donnant un nom avec lequel ils devront former un nouveau nom.

e.g. **Équipe 1 :** *butter* **Équipe 2 :** *butterfly!*

Je prononce

A L'intonation des questions en *WH-*

a. **Écoute des questions.** Track 82
Sur quel(s) mot(s) l'intonation monte-t-elle ? À la fin de la question, est-elle montante ou descendante ?

b. **Par quels mots commencent ces questions ?**

c. **Écoute d'autres questions.** Track 83
Compare leur intonation avec celle des questions précédentes. Que remarques-tu ?

d. **Répète ces phrases en respectant bien l'intonation.**

B L'accentuation des mots composés

a. **Écoute les mots suivants.** Track 84
treasure island – eye patch – nickname – shipwreck – pegleg – daylight
Comment sont-ils accentués ?

b. **Écoute à présent ces deux phrases.** Track 85
Blackbeard is scary. He's got a black beard.
Entends-tu la différence d'accentuation des mots soulignés ?

c. **Répète ces mots et ces phrases en t'enregistrant puis compare avec le modèle.**

Have fun with...

Pirate Language

1 Find out your pirate name

To become a real pirate, you need a pirate name!

Use the pirate name generator!

http://pirate.namegeneratorfun.com/

2 Learn how to speak like a pirate

No treasure for **you**!	No treasure for **ye**!
We're sail**ing**	We're sail**in'**
Yes!	**Aye**!
Make **him** walk the plank!	Make **'im** walk the plank!
Red	**Rrrrrred**

(roll the "r")

3 Make sure you understand pirates

ahoy	→	hello/ Hey!
aye	→	yes
fair winds!	→	good luck!
matey	→	friend
sail ho!	→	I see a ship!

avast	→	stop
booty	→	treasure
scallywag	→	a bad person
scurvy dog!	→	*a fine insult*
yo-ho-ho	→	*pirate laughter*

I Dare you **Listen to Mad Cap'n Sally "Dog Rough" Bones and try to decipher her message!** Track 86a

DRAMA CLUB

presents

CHARACTERS

- Captain
- Pirate 1
- Pirate 2
- Pirate 3
- Scallywag

Walking The Plank

CAPTAIN:
Bring out the dirty scallywag who ate the ship's food!!

PIRATE 1:
Arr, Cap'n! Here 'e is!

PIRATE 2:
Make 'im walk the plank, Cap'n!

PIRATE 3:
Aye! Walk the plank! Give 'im to the fishes! We are five hundred miles from land and not even a biscuit to eat!

CAPTAIN:
What's that? No biscuits left? *Throw 'im off the ship!*

SCALLYWAG:
Whoa... wait! Wait! Parlay! Parlay*!

CAPTAIN:
What, Scallywag? Got somethin' to say before we feed you to the sharks?

SCALLYWAG:
I promise, Cap'n... I didn't want to eat all your biscuits. But I'm a little... bit... drunk.

PIRATE 1:
Aye! That's not surprising, Cap'n! 'E finished your rum as well!

CAPTAIN:
My rum? Wh.. which bottle? You're not talkin' about my *special* rum, are ye?

PIRATE 2:
Aye, Cap'n. The bottle you were keepin' for Christmas!

CAPTAIN:
Thunderation! Give me my cutlass!

SCALLYWAG:
Wait! *Pa-pa-parlay!* PARLAAAY!!
Cap'n... we need to 'ave a *little* parlay about the treasure.

CAPTAIN:
There'll be no treasure for *ye*,
ye pox-popping popinjay!

SCALLYWAG:
Hum... well there'll be no treasure for you either, Cap'n!

CAPTAIN:
What? What's that, Scallywag?

SCALLYWAG:
Well, I ate the treasure map as well...

* *From the French "parler"*

AUDIO
86 b

- **Listen to the scene, then rehearse it.**
  ☺ Use p. 84 for help.
- **Act out the scene.**

Ready for the test?

ACCOMPAGNEMENT PERSONNALISÉ AP

Révise | **Entraîne-toi**

Compréhension de l'oral

Réécoute

AUDIO 69

Écoute quelqu'un parler de la célèbre pirate, Anne Bonny

AUDIO 87

- À quel type d'informations t'attends-tu ?
- Écoute, puis explique ce que tu as compris, au choix : par des mots ou des phrases / en anglais ou en français / par des dessins / …
- Explique-le maintenant par écrit en français.
- Compare avec un camarade et discutez-en. Quelles stratégies avez-vous utilisées ?

Expression orale

Exprime-toi sur le thème des pirates

→ Réécoute la description de la carte au trésor (p. 77) et essaie d'imiter la personne qui parle.

Track 71

Échange avec un camarade

- Choisis un nouvel emplacement pour le trésor sur la carte dans ton *workbook* p. 77. Explique à ton camarade comment s'y rendre. Il devra dessiner le chemin. Échangez ensuite les rôles.
- Comment améliorer vos performances ?
  - donner plus de détails ?
  - utiliser un vocabulaire plus précis ?
  - quelques connecteurs ?
  - mieux prononcer les sons /eɪ/ et /aɪ/ ?
  - … ?

Compréhension de l'écrit

Relis

→ L'infographie pp. 74-75 et le texte p. 76

Lis la suite du roman p. 76

- Tu peux feuilleter quelques pages du roman de Caroline Carlson sur www.amazon.com
- Lis aussi les pages *Get better at reading* p. 131.

Expression écrite

Relis

→ Tes leçons

→ Les Time to write dans ton *workbook*

→ How to fill in a form p. 79

→ Les Training tasks p. 75 et 77

Avec tes camarades :

- Rédige un nouveau formulaire d'inscription pour postuler à ta prochaine expédition sur l'île au trésor et soumets-le à un camarade.
- Puis, remplis celui qu'il va te donner !

+ Imagine ce que le professeur pourra te demander dans chaque test

CHAPITRE FLASH

Legend

King Arthur

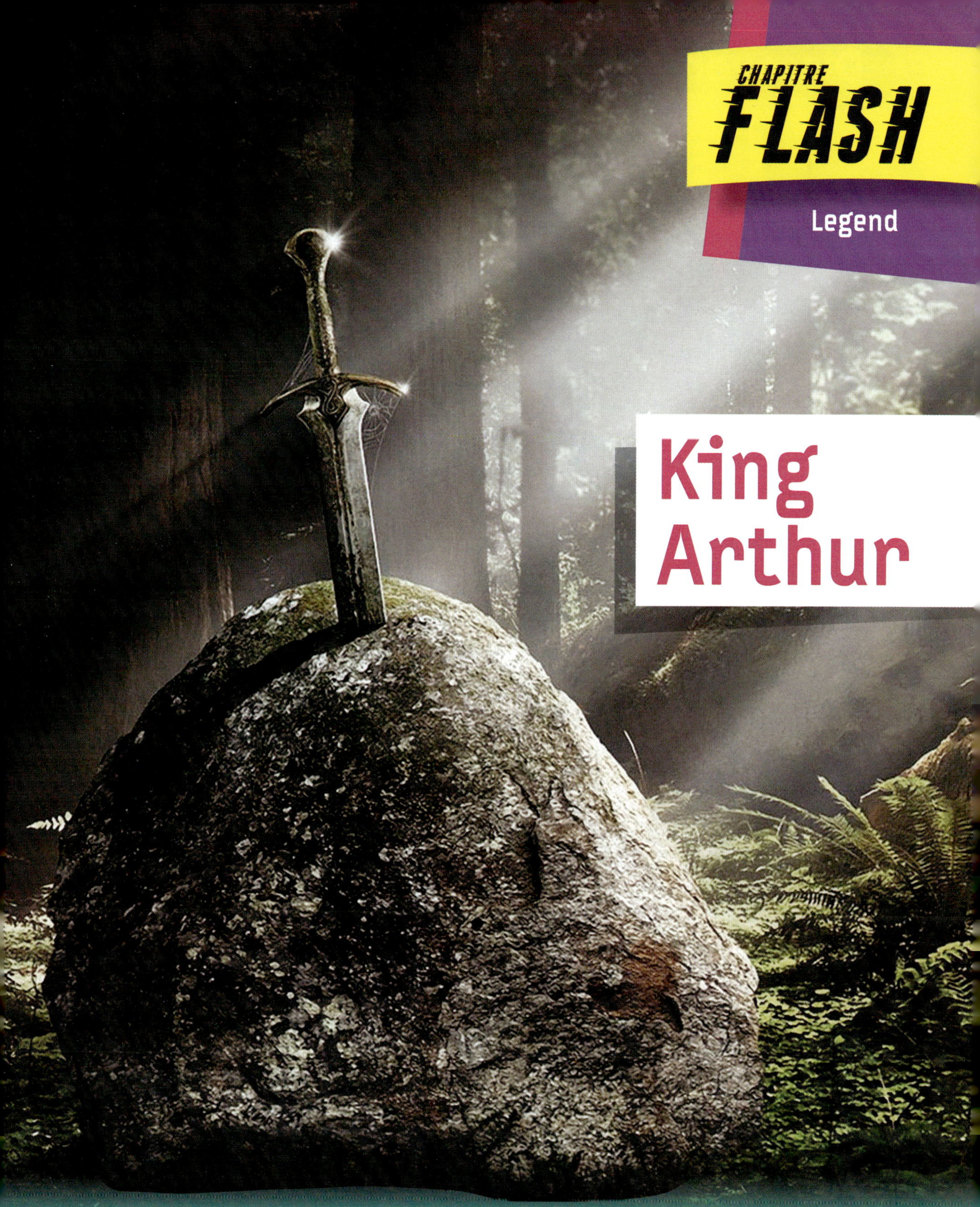

AUDIO 88

Flash interview:

If we say "hero" and "sword", who do you think of?

MINI PROJECT

Tell the story of a heroic character.

EPI > Anglais - Français - Histoire :
LE CHEVALIER, UN HÉROS INTEMPOREL ?

Discover

The Legend

King Arthur

AUDIO 89 The Legend of King Arthur

i Dare you **In groups, design the comic book pages just before and just after this one.**

King Arthur - Excalibur Unsheathed: An English Legend

1. **Look.** Do you recognize this scene?
2. **You are going to listen to this boy's story.** Note down what you expect:
   characters *time* *place* *events*
3. **Listen to the story**:
   a. Part 1
   b. Part 2
   c. Part 3
   → Say what you understand and complete your notes from question 2.

Tip

- Écoute bien la **musique**, elle t'aidera à situer l'époque à laquelle se déroulent ces faits.
- Appuie-toi sur les **connecteurs logiques** pour suivre le déroulement de l'histoire.

4. **Time to write!** Complete the comic book page above with:
   speech balloons *thought balloons* *sound effects* *captions* → WB p. 96
5. Listen and discover more about the characters. Track 90 → WB p. 97
6. Discuss the legend: what makes Arthur a hero?

King Arthur's heritage

1

At the end of the second book of the Harry Potter *saga, Harry has to defeat the Basilisk, a giant snake, and save Ginny. Without a weapon or a wand, Harry fears the worst. All of a sudden, something unexpected happens…*

"A gleaming silver sword had appeared inside the hat…"

2

"Only a true Gryffindor could have pulled that out of the hat, Harry," said Dumbledore simply.

Harry Potter and the Chamber of Secrets, J.K. Rowling, 1998

1 **Look at the pictures.** Do you know these characters?

2 a. **Read text 1** and use it to label the pictures. → WB p. 98

b. **Read text 2** and compare Harry Potter's adventure with the myth of King Arthur. Can you see similarities?

3 **Time to write!** Rewrite Dumbledore's quote to apply it to Arthur. → WB p. 98

4 Listen to a summary of Harry Potter's adventures and find more similarities.
Track 91

Tip

- **Réécoute** les documents audio Tracks 89 et 91.
- **Prépare des notes** efficaces (mots-clefs, structure du récit).
- **Enregistre-toi.** Plusieurs fois seront peut-être nécessaires.
- Pense à bien **mettre le ton** et fais attention à la **prononciation**.

MINI PROJECT

Tell the story of a heroic character

In groups

WORK YOUR WAY

Choose an existing character.

or Create your own Arthurian/heroic character.

- Think about his/her:

identity | *qualities and skills* | *family story* | *mentor* | *friends* | *magic weapon* | …

- Record your character's story and share it on a Padlet wall dedicated to "the heritage of King Arthur".

GRAMMAIRE

- Le génitif • Le superlatif → WB p. 100/102

Language tools

Apprends ces mots avec leur prononciation !

Words

Heroic qualities

Track 92

honorable
/ɒ/

brave / cou**ra**geous
/kəˈreɪdʒəs/

ad**ven**turous
/adˈvɜntʃərəs/

strong

kind/nice

de**ter**mined

Time and Setting

Track 94

kingdom
/ə/

tower
/aʊ/

manor
= **cas**tle
/kɑːsəl/

dungeon

the Dark **A**ges / the **Mi**ddle **A**ges / Me**die**val times

People

Track 93

king / queen

prince / **prin**cess

lord / **la**dy

knight
/naɪt/

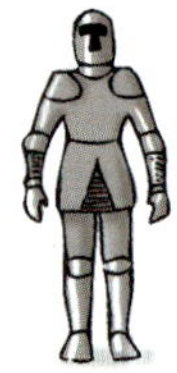

armour

wizard
/ə/

sword
/sɔːd/

lance

tournament
/tʊənəmənt/

Grammar

J'établis des liens grâce au génitif

1. **Merlin's magic and wisdom** protected Arthur.
2. Arthur was **Pendragon's son**.

Pour établir des liens entre deux noms (personnes ou choses), on utilise le plus souvent le génitif (**'s**) : ***Merlin's magic***

Nom 1 ╳ Nom 2

La magie de Merlin

J'utilise le superlatif de supériorité

1. You will be **the greatest** king of all.
2. Arthur is a good king, **the best** England has ever had.
3. Merlin is **the most powerful** magician in England.

Pour dire qu'un élément est supérieur, dans un domaine, à un groupe, on utilise le superlatif de supériorité.

(!) **Construction :** *the* + adjectif court* + *(e)st*
ou *the* + *most* + adjectif long*

* Voir p. 100

(!) Pluriels

Quand le nom est au pluriel terminé par **-s**, on n'écrit que l'apostrophe :

my parents' bedroom

(!) Cas particuliers

- Adjectifs de deux syllabes terminés en ***-y*** :
  happy → *the happ**iest***
- Certains adjectifs ont un superlatif **irrégulier** :
  good → ***the best*** *bad* → ***the worst***
  far → ***the farthest/the furthest***

Track 151
Fast, faster, fastest
with Fluency MC

+ Exercices

→ WB p. 99-104

Project 6

Robots

AUDIO 95

Flash interview:

What does the word "robot" evoke for you?

Training Tasks

- What robot are you?
- Write about the future!

FINAL TASK

- In teams, take part in a robotics competition!

Discover

Awesome robots

AUDIO
96
Annie talks about famous robots

Spot the robot!

1

2

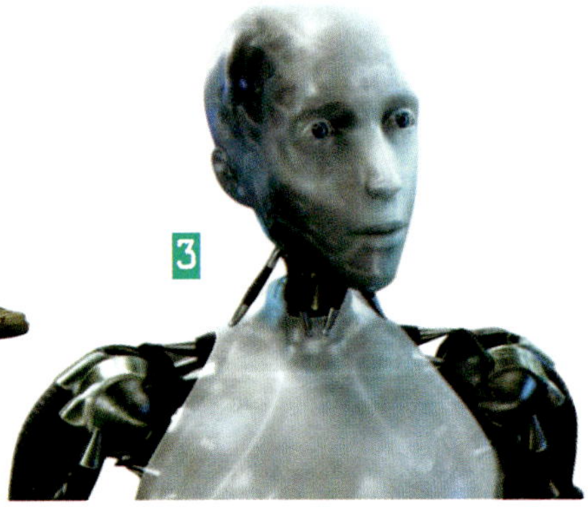

3

4

1. **Here are some famous robots.** Do you know any of them?
2. **Listen to part 1 and play "who's who?".** Spot the robots.
3. **Listen to part 2 and discover Annie's favourite robot.** Do you understand why she likes it best?
4. **Which robot do *you* like best?**
   a. Get ready to explain why:
   personality | *skills* | *shape* | *colours* | ...
   b. Share with your classmates.
5. **Time to write!** Which robot had the most success? Write a short paragraph about him or her.

Tip

Pour **exprimer tes préférences**, tu peux reprendre des expressions employées par Annie mais tu peux aussi te servir du vocabulaire que tu connais déjà.

Your personal healthcare companion

VIDEO 5 Watch an extract from the film *Big Hero 6*

How to speak with someone p. 97.

1. **Look at the picture.** What do you expect in the movie scene?

place | *characters* | *situation* | ...

2. **Watch the extract.** Use it to complete Baymax's information card. → WB p. 105

3. **a. "On a scale of 1 to 10", how useful do you think Baymax is?**
Think about his:

role | *personality* | *appearance*

b. Compare Baymax with the robots on p. 92.

4. **Time to write!** You are the creator of Baymax. Write a short text to present your amazing creation.

Tip
Utilise tes réponses aux questions 2 et 3 pour préparer ton **paragraphe** sur Baymax.

Training Task

What robot are you?

- Choose one of the robots in your workbook. → WB p. 105
- Imagine you are this robot. Just like Baymax, introduce yourself to the class:

your name | *your abilities* | *your role*

Need help? → WB p. 106

GRAMMAIRE
- Le comparatif → WB p. 111

TN Robot battle!

The future

What will the future be like?

Elon University School of Communications

Home

Predictions Surveys

KidZone

About the Site

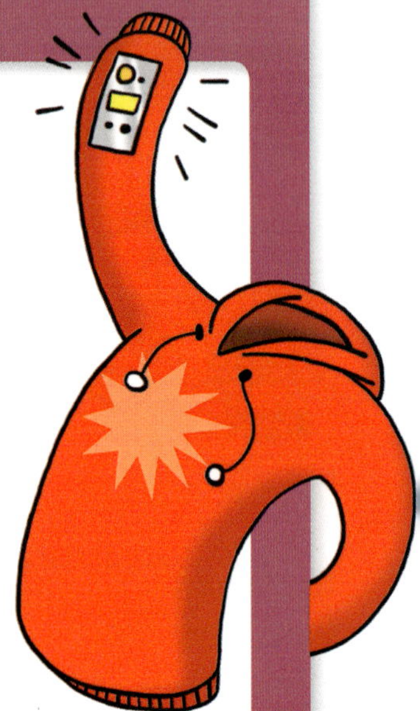

Kids' Predictions for Our Future

We asked fifth-graders at Elon Elementary School in North Carolina to write what they think the future will bring. Read some of their ideas, and then write about what you think will happen! Share your ideas with your classmates, friends and family. You never know; they might come true sooner than you think.

Amanda F. – In the future there will be hoverboards, flying cars and pocket-size computers.

Sydney Y. – We will have robots that clean up after us. The X-box game will be so small it will fit in your watch. Time machines will be amazing.

Jordan W. – There will be enough technology so we can communicate with aliens. There will be a time machine to travel through time. There will be the power to die and come back alive.

Danielle M. – There will be a remote[1] where you type in where you want to go then push the button and you will be there. Also we will have chewing gum that never loses its taste.

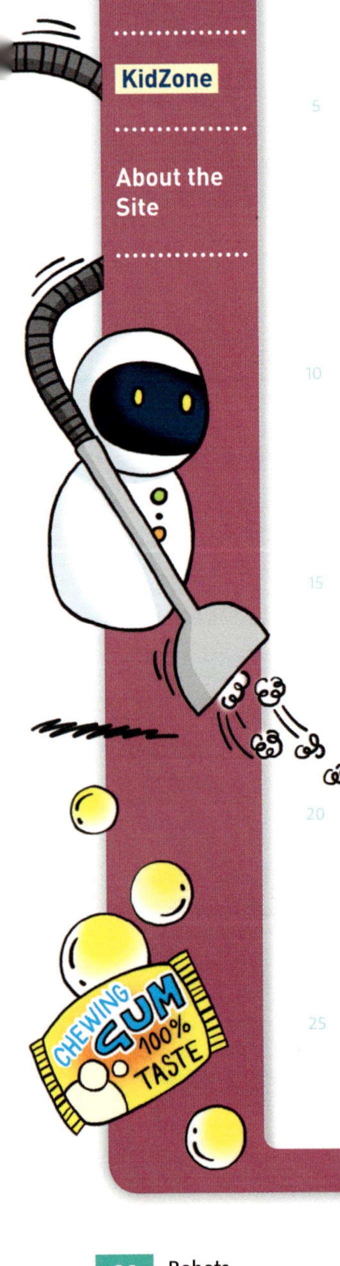

Patrick D. – There will be robots that clean your house, walk the dog, make your bed and stuff like that. There will be computers so small you can't see them.

Hannah P. – We will have mini-computers in our clothes – like on the inside of your sleeves. You will also be able to type into your hairbrush how you want your hair to be styled. Robots can get everything for you because you can tell them to make you something.

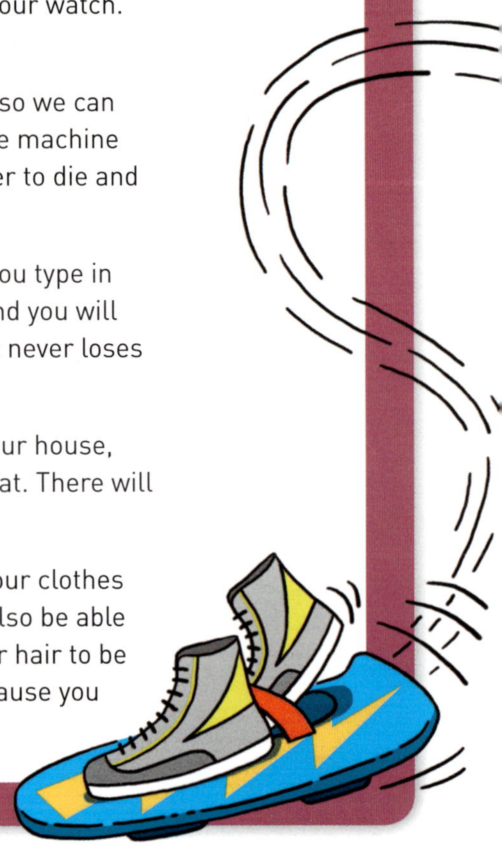

1. *télécommande*

www. elon.edu

1 **Read the title of the document and the introduction.** Identify the situation:

> **Kids' Predictions for Our Future**
> We asked fifth-graders at Elon Elementary School in North Carolina to write what they think the future will bring.

2 **a. Work in pairs. Read at least two comments and identify the predictions.** → WB p. 106

> **Tip**
> Appuie-toi sur la présence de *will* pour **repérer les prédictions**.

b. React. In your opinion, are these predictions realistic 👍 or unrealistic 👎? Explain why.

3 **In groups** Join another pair of classmates and discuss the comments you have read: any common points? Differences?

4 **Time to write!** Complete the spidergram with your favourite predictions:

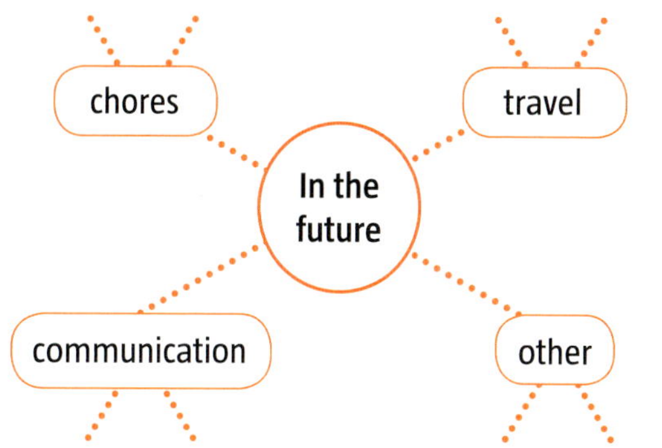

→ WB p. 107

Training Task

Write about the future!

- As the website suggested, now write about what *you* think will happen:

at work | *at home* | *at school* | ... → WB p. 108

- Share your ideas with your friends and family: post them on a Padlet wall.

> **Tip**
> N'hésite pas à **reprendre des expressions et des structures** employées dans les témoignages.

GRAMMAIRE
- *Will* → WB p. 114

FINAL TASK

Design a robot!

In teams, take part in a robotics competiton.

1 Get ready

Work in teams

- **Discover the competition!**

Watch the video to understand what *FIRST* is.

VIDEO 6 "It's really fun!"

- **Design your robot**

– Decide **why** you will need a robot.

– Prepare your notes about your robot:

its appearance | *its name* | *what it will be able to do* | *how it will improve people's lives*

– Use this website to design your robot and fill in the form with your notes. →

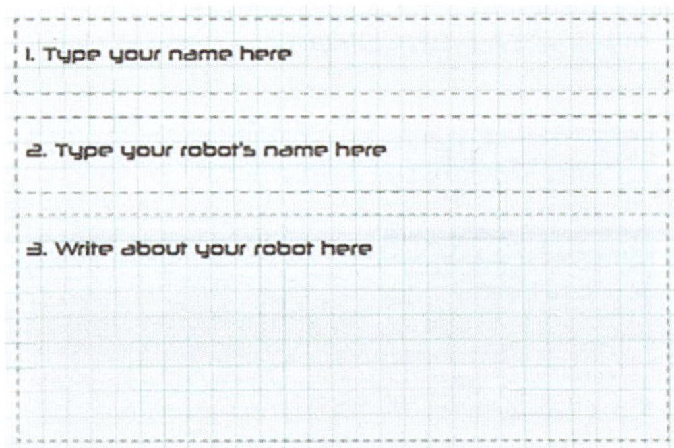
1. Type your name here
2. Type your robot's name here
3. Write about your robot here

www.abcya.com/make_a_robot.htm

2 Action!

- **Present your robot to the class. Who wins?**
- **Make your presentation interactive:**

Tip

- Pour présenter ton robot, tu peux utiliser les notes que tu as entrées dans le **formulaire en ligne**.
- Tes notes doivent êtres succinctes : quelques **mots-clé**.

Describe your robot.
→ Your classmate will draw it!

or

Show 3 different robots to the class.
→ Your classmates will listen to your description and spot your robot.

or

Present your robot.
→ Make the class guess his/her name. Who wins?

I bet his name is...

How to...
Speak with someone *even a robot!*

ACCOMPAGNEMENT AP PERSONNALISÉ

Pour mener une conversation, il faut bien écouter et savoir réagir.

Réécoute attentivement les premiers échanges entre **Baymax** et **Hiro**. Video 5

1 ***Hello**! I am Baymax, your personal healthcare companion.*

2 *Er... **Hey**! Baymax... I didn't know you were still active...*

3 ***What** seems to be the trouble?*

4 *Oh... **I just stubbed my toe a little, I'm fine**.*

5 *On a scale of 1 to 10, **how** would you rate your pain?*

6 *Er... Zero? **I'm okay, really, thanks.***

Pour bien échanger avec ton interlocuteur, il faut bien l'écouter !

__Does__ it __hurt__ when I __touch__ it?

Appuie-toi sur :

– Les **mots accentués**, porteurs de sens.

– L'intonation, le ton, l'accent de phrase qui peuvent donner des indications sur les sentiments de ton interlocuteur et la nature de la phrase (question, exclamation...).

Laisse-toi le temps de réfléchir

Utilise des *gap-fillers* (des mots et expressions qui pourront t'être utiles pour t'exprimer naturellement ou pour gagner du temps quand tu ne sais pas quoi dire.)

– Hiro en utilise : relève-les dans ses réponses ci-dessus et entraîne-toi à les dire.

– Écoutes-en d'autres et entraîne-toi à les employer en imaginant des contextes. Track 97

Sois poli(e) avec ton interlocuteur

Utilise des formules de politesse

Lesquelles utilisent Baymax et Hiro ? En connais-tu d'autres ?

À toi de jouer !

1. Baymax a évolué ! Il peut maintenant prendre en compte les réponses de son patient. Rejoue la scène avec un camarade en adaptant les répliques de chacun à cette évolution.
2. Dialogue avec C-Ted ! Écoute-le et réponds-lui. Track 98

Words

Apprends ces mots avec leur prononciation !

Humans & robots

Body parts
Track 99

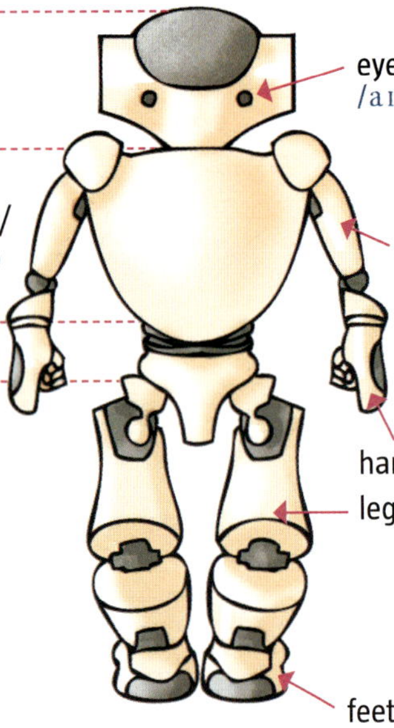

Personality traits
Track 100

helpful

effi**ci**ent
/ʃ/

o**be**dient
/biː/

tireless
/taɪə/

awesome = great = a**ma**zing
/ˈɔːsəm/

patient

caring

re**li**able
/aɪə/

Chores
Track 101

chores = tasks
/tʃɔːrz/

vacuum the floor
/vækjuːm/

do the **clea**ning

tidy up
your room

make the bed

set the **ta**ble ≠ clear the **ta**ble

carry the
shopping

wash the **di**shes

take out the trash (US) /
the bin (UK)

make **din**ner

Advantages 🙂
Track 102

im**prove** daily life
/uː/
make life **ea**sier
save time
help with the **gar**dening / the **coo**king
o**bey** your orders / o**bey** you
take care of = look **af**ter

Risks ☹
Track 103

take **peo**ple's jobs
re**place** **hu**mans

+

Learn these words in your workbook

→ WB p. 109

→ More exercises in your WB p. 110

Je m'entraîne

1 **Es-tu plus perspicace qu'un robot ? Trouve l'intrus dans chaque série et remplace-le par un mot ou une expression plus appropriés.**

1. improve daily life – save time – take people's jobs

2. play – tidy – wash the dishes

3. mouth – nose – leg

4. awful – amazing – awesome

2 **Work with a friend. Dis un mot du chapitre, ton camarade devra le répéter puis en donner un autre. À ton tour, répète les deux mots puis ajoutes-en un 3e, et ainsi de suite jusqu'à atteindre 15 mots. Tiendrez-vous jusqu'au bout ?**

3 **Présente ce robot :**

body parts

skills

advantages

…

4 **Ton robot s'active dans la maison ! Écoute des sons et identifie les tâches ménagères qu'il est en train d'accomplir.** Track 104

5 **Work with a friend. Joue au Scrabble avec les mots du chapitre.**

6 **Réécris ces phrases en utilisant des verbes de ta leçon.**

1. Robots can make people's lives better.

2. They can look after children and elderly people.

3. They can help you have more time for yourself.

4. They do whatever you ask them to.

Je prononce

A **Comme un Anglophone !** Track 105

a. Écoute ces interjections :

ow – wow – ouch – yum – oops – phew – yuck – gee – oh – er

b. Que signifient-elles d'après toi ?

c. Entraîne-toi à les répéter, puis enregistre-toi et compare avec le modèle.

B **Les sons /əʊ/, /ɒ/ et /ɔː/** Track 106

a. Écoute les mots suivants, en faisant attention à la prononciation de [o] :

robot – devoted – drop – chores – torso – nose – body – autonomous – organize

b. Classe ces mots selon la prononciation de [o] :

/əʊ/	/ɒ/	/ɔː/
…	…	…

c. Entraîne-toi à les prononcer.

VIDEO

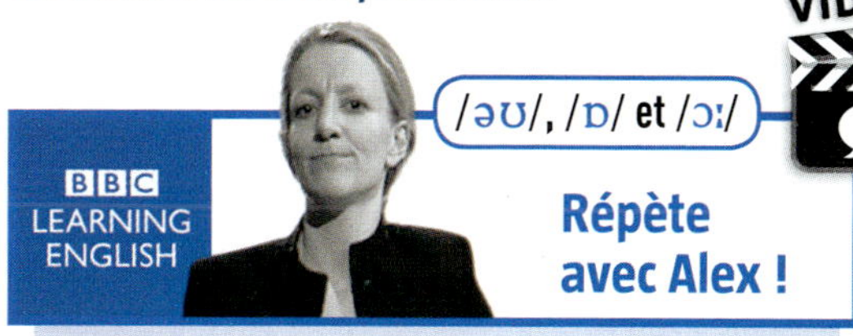

i Dare you **Twist your tongue!**

"Rob is not a robot because Rob has a boat while a robot does not."

Grammar

Les projets de la robotique nous incitent à comparer hier et aujourd'hui, ou tel robot et tel autre, mais aussi à envisager l'avenir.

1. Je compare

This robot is **better than** the others: it is **bigger**, **more helpful** and **less fragile than** they are. Plus, it is **as intelligent as** humans.

Si l'on veut comparer des **éléments** ou des **personnes**, on peut utiliser :

	Construction
Le comparatif de supériorité	adjectif court + -(e)r + *than* ou *more* + adjectif long + *than*
Le comparatif d'infériorité	*less* + adjectif + *than*
Le comparatif d'égalité	*as* + adjectif + *as*

Adjectifs :

- Les adjectifs d'**une syllabe** sont considérés comme **courts**.
- La plupart des adjectifs de **deux syllabes** ou plus sont considérés comme **longs**.
- Certains adjectifs de **deux syllabes**, notamment ceux qui se terminent par -***y*** et -***er*** et -***ow***, fonctionnent souvent comme des adjectifs courts.
  Exemples :
  lazy → lazier; *clever → cleverer*

(!) Certains adjectifs ont un comparatif de supériorité **irrégulier**.
Exemples : *good → better* *bad → worse* *far → further*

Track 151
Fast, faster, fastest
with Fluency MC

2. Je parle de l'avenir avec *will*

1. *Robots **will** **replace** humans.*
2. ***Will** they also **do** our homework?*
3. *No, they **won't**...!*

- Avec *WILL*, on fait des prédictions qu'on imagine comme très probables.
- Attention, comme *CAN* par exemple, *WILL* est un auxiliaire modal.
  Il est donc soumis à **3 règles d'or** :

Il est toujours suivi d'un verbe à l'infinitif

Il est invariable

Il ne peut être ni suivi, ni précédé d'un autre modal : c'est par exemple pour cela qu'on a besoin de ***be able to***.

- Construction :

– Phrase affirmative (1) : sujet + *will* + infinitif du verbe
– Phrase interrogative (2) : *will* + sujet + infinitif du verbe
– Phrase négative (3) : sujet + [*will* + ***not*** + infinitif du verbe / *won't*]

Track 152
I can, I will, I must
with Fluency MC

→ More exercises in your WB p. 113-116

Je m'entraîne

→ Je compare

1 Et si tu essayais de convaincre tes parents d'acheter un robot pour la maison ?
Tu peux utiliser les adjectifs suivants :

nervous – organised – quick – tired – obedient

e.g. *A robot can drive better than you because it will be less nervous.*

2 Compare ces deux robots.

Wall - E

Transformer

Tu peux utiliser les verbes : *be* | *look* | *seem*
et les adjectifs :

small | *impressive* | *aggressive* | *old* | *technically advanced* | *efficient* | *modern*

3 Écoute quelqu'un parler d'un robot et dessine-le.
Sais-tu de quel robot il s'agit ? Track 107

4 Complète ce témoignage :

Life in 2030 will be (fascinating) than today and it will also be (easy). Everybody will live in (modern) flats than they do now. So, everything will be (comfortable). We will certainly have (efficient) appliances, like robots. We will not work (much) as today, so our lives will be (tiring).

→ Je parle de l'avenir

5 Tu viens de commander un robot sur Internet, imagine ce que tu vas faire de ton temps libre une fois qu'il sera là pour t'aider !
e.g. *I will have more time to read.*

6 Un androïde a été créé pour toi. Tu vas pouvoir l'envoyer en cours à ta place ! Programme-le de façon à ce qu'aucun professeur ne s'en rende compte.
e.g. *In Geography, you will draw maps very quickly.*

in PE | *in foreign languages* | *in French* | *in history* | *in mathematics*

7 a. Complète les pages « *Predict your future* » de *Diary of a Wimpy Kid*. → WB p. 117

b. Imagine deux autres prédictions. Propose à ton voisin de classe de les compléter !

8 Avec un camarade, imagine 5 inventions du futur.
e. g. *In the future, there will be flying cars.*

Je prononce

Le comparatif de supériorité Track 108

a. Écoute les phrases suivantes en faisant bien attention à la prononciation des mots en gras.

1. This robot is **smaller** and **better** than the others.

Comparatif suivi d'une voyelle : on prononce le « r » car on fait la liaison

Comparatif suivi d'une consonne : on ne prononce pas le « r » car on ne fait pas la liaison

2. This robot is **more** intelligent and **more** helpful.

b. Entraîne-toi à bien prononcer ces phrases.

Have fun with...

DIARY of a Wimpy Kid

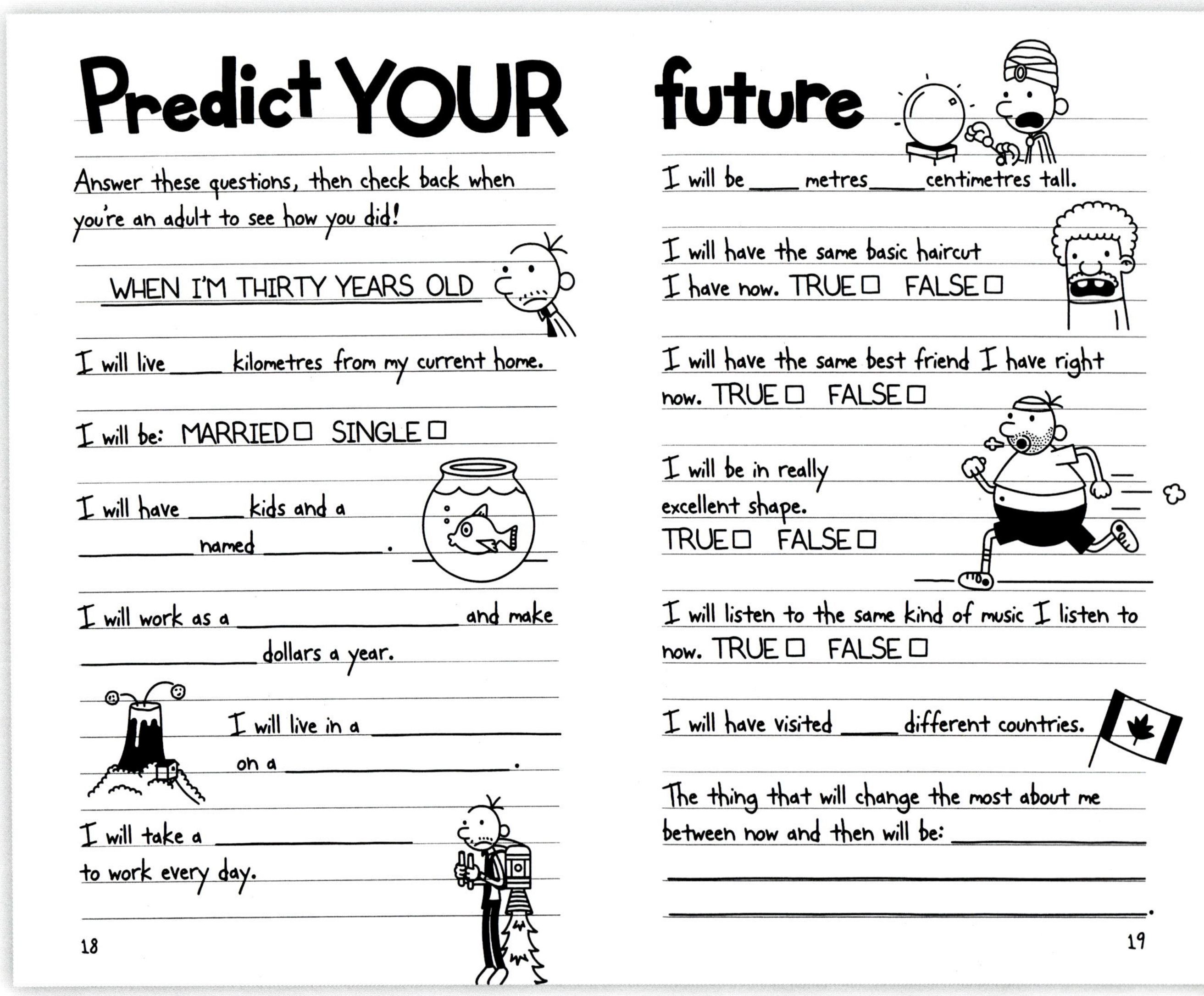

Predict YOUR future

Answer these questions, then check back when you're an adult to see how you did!

WHEN I'M THIRTY YEARS OLD

I will live ____ kilometres from my current home.

I will be: MARRIED ☐ SINGLE ☐

I will have ____ kids and a __________ named __________.

I will work as a ______________ and make ____________ dollars a year.

I will live in a ____________ on a ____________.

I will take a ____________ to work every day.

18

I will be ___ metres ____ centimetres tall.

I will have the same basic haircut I have now. TRUE ☐ FALSE ☐

I will have the same best friend I have right now. TRUE ☐ FALSE ☐

I will be in really excellent shape. TRUE ☐ FALSE ☐

I will listen to the same kind of music I listen to now. TRUE ☐ FALSE ☐

I will have visited ____ different countries.

The thing that will change the most about me between now and then will be: ______________________________

19

→ WB p. 117

Diary of a Wimpy Kid: Do-It-Yourself, Jeff Kinney, 2011

I Dare you **Close your eyes and ask a friend to pick one workbook in the class for you. Read the predictions and guess whose workbook it is. Explain why.**

DRAMA CLUB

presents

CHARACTERS
- Mary
- Oliver
- Jojo

The Brownie Recipe

MARY:
Is there anything to eat in your house? I'm really hungry.

OLIVER:
Me too. But the fridge is empty.

MARY:
That's okay – we can make something!

OLIVER:
Like... brownies? Do you know how?

MARY:
No... but my phone does! Hey, Jojo, how do you make brownies?

JOJO:
I'm sorry, Mary, I don't understand. Please repeat the question.

MARY:
How... Do... Brow-nies?

JOJO:
...did you say 'Ow! Two blue knees!', Mary?

OLIVER:
No, she said brownies. With chocolate!

MARY:
We are hungry!

JOJO:
I'm sorry to hear that you are angry, Mary. Can I help?

OLIVER:
No, not 'angry' – hungry! We are very... *hungry*!

JOJO:
Here is what I have found on the web about... Hungary.

MARY:
Hungary! *Why don't you work?*

JOJO:
Here is a route to... 'Walk to Hungary'.

MARY:
Shut up, you stupid machine! *We don't want to walk to Hungary!* We are hungry!

OLIVER:
Yes! *Hungry*, see?

JOJO:
Searching for 'Hungary... by sea'. I'm sorry, Mary, but it seems Hungary is not accessible by sea. Would you like me to check on train times instead?

AUDIO 109

- **Listen to the scene, then rehearse it.**
- **Act out the scene.**

Ready for the test?

ACCOMPAGNEMENT AP PERSONNALISÉ

	Révise	Entraîne-toi
Compréhension de l'oral	**Réécoute** AUDIO 96	**Écoute et devine le nom du robot** AUDIO 110 • Explique ce que tu as compris, au choix : par des mots ou des phrases / en anglais ou en français / par des dessins / ... • Explique-le maintenant par écrit en français. • Compare avec un camarade et discutez-en.
Expression orale	**Exprime-toi** sur le thème des robots → **Training task** p. 93. → Relis **How to speak with someone** p. 97. → Enregistre-toi et écoute. Es-tu satisfait(e) ?	**Échange avec tes camarades** • Ton robot domestique préféré a préparé une salade avec les plantes vertes de la maison ! Tes parents veulent en changer, mais tu n'es pas d'accord. Répartissez les rôles et discutez ! • Comment améliorer vos performances ? utiliser un vocabulaire précis pour parler des traits de caractère, des corvées... ? / utiliser les comparatifs ? / quelques connecteurs ? / ...
Compréhension de l'écrit	**Relis** → Le texte p. 94	**Essaie de lire d'autres prédictions** • Regarde sur le site www.elon.edu/e-web/predictions/kidzone/yourfuture.xhtml En bas de la page, tu trouveras une section intitulée *Kids' predictions for our future*. • Échange avec un camarade : laquelle as-tu trouvé la plus intéressante, farfelue ou réaliste ?
Expression écrite	**Relis** → Le **Time to write** p. 95 → La **Training task** p. 95	**Qu'en pensent les robots ?** • Rédige les prédictions d'un robot pour la page *Robots' predictions for the future*. • Comment améliorer ta production : donner plus de détails ? / bien utiliser les comparatifs ? / faire attention à l'expression du futur ? / ...

+ Imagine ce que le professeur pourra te demander dans chaque test

CHAPITRE FLASH

Storytelling

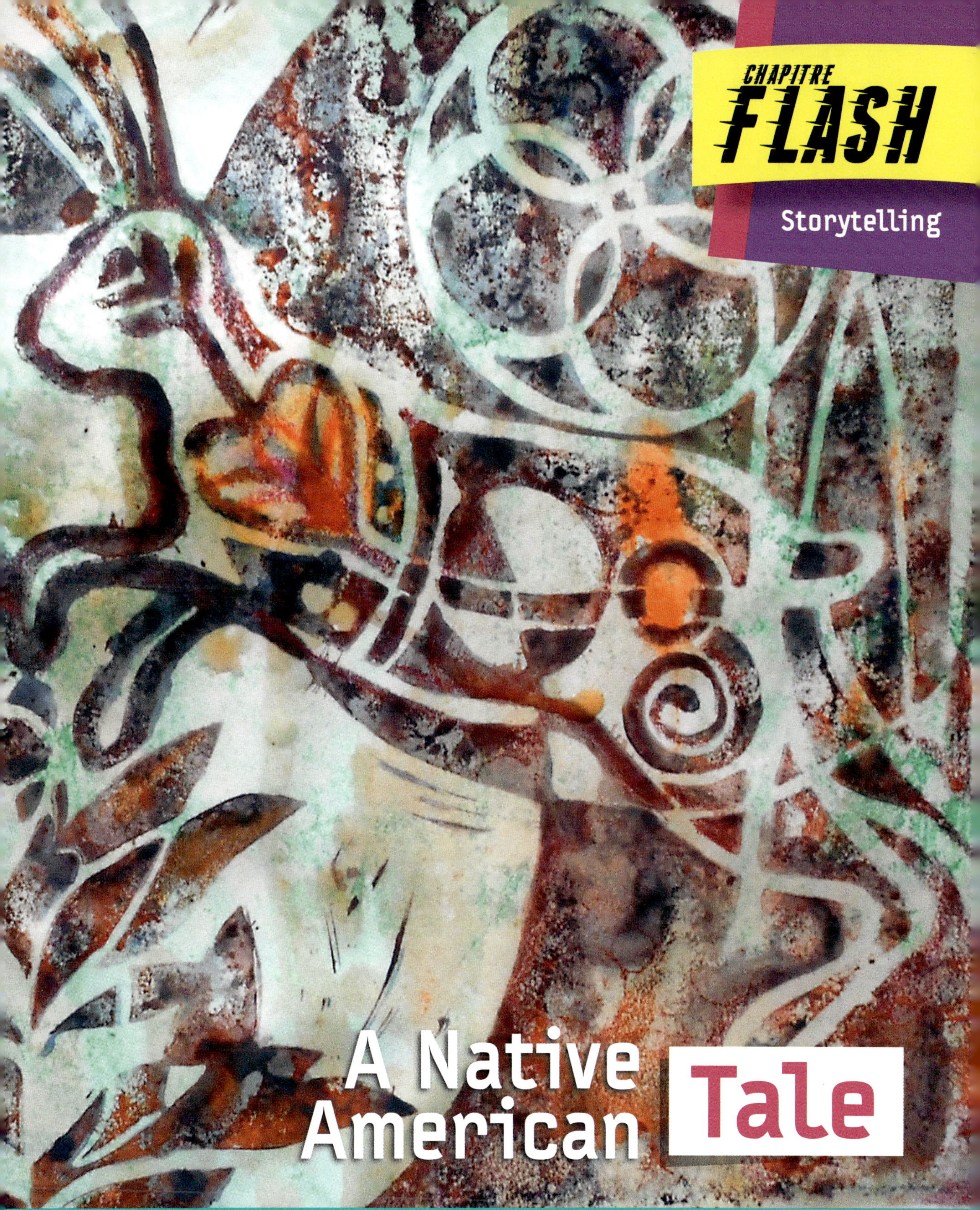

A Native American Tale

AUDIO 111

Flash interview:
What is your favourite tale?

MINI PROJECT

Tell us a story!

EPI > Anglais - Français : RACONTE-MOI LE MONDE

Discover

A Native American myth

Meet a storyteller

VIDEO 7 Meet Grayhawk Perkins

Grayhawk Perkins is a Native American singer and storyteller from Louisiana.

1. **You are going to watch Grayhawk Perkins introduce himself.** What kind of information can you expect? Note it down.
2. **Watch part 1 of the video and meet Grayhawk.**
   a. Check ✓ or cross out ✗ your guesses.
   b. Watch again and complete your notes.
   c. Use what you have learnt to label the map in your workbook. → WB p. 118
3. **Watch part 2.** Some words are repeated and stressed. Can you hear them? What do they reveal about Grayhawk's childhood?
4. **Time to write!** Fill in Grayhawk's profile. → WB p. 118

Native Americans

They are the first people who lived in the US, long before the arrival of Christopher Columbus and the Europeans. They were grouped into tribes or nations all over the country, each one with its religion, customs and language.

Listen to a legend

VIDEO 8

Grayhawk tells a creation myth:
How The Alligator Got His Skin

1 Read the title of the legend:

How the Alligator Got his Skin

Why is it called a "creation myth"?

2 Listen to the first sentences of the story. Raise your hand when you hear words from the title.

3 a. Watch part 1. Complete the illustration in your workbook. → WB p. 119

b. What do you expect next?

Tip

Appuie-toi sur les **gestes** et les **expressions** de Grayhawk.

4 a. Watch part 2. Complete your illustration with:

the new characters | *speech bubbles* | *the emotions of the characters* → WB p. 119

b. What do you expect next?

5 Time to write!

Imagine and write the end of the story.

6 How is a creation myth structured? Complete the diagram in your workbook. → WB p. 120

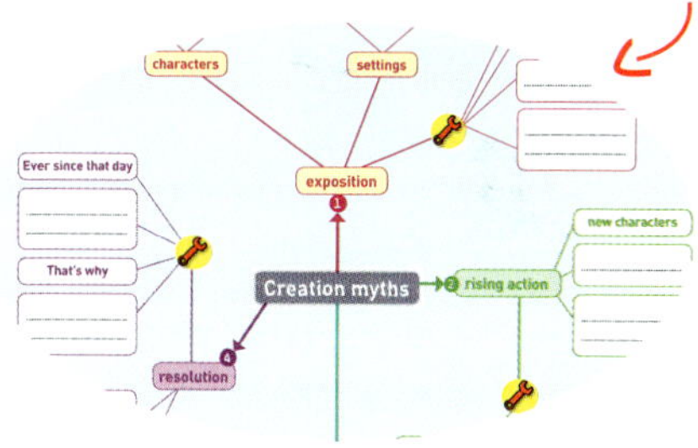

MINI PROJECT

Tell us a story!

In groups

WORK YOUR WAY

Act out Grayhawk's tale **or** Imagine a new tale and act it out

How the Raccoon Got his Striped Tail

How the Buffalo Got his Hump

How the Porcupine Got his Quills

- Choose the actors: *the storyteller* | *the animals*
- Discuss the staging and practise telling the story.
- Act out the story!

Tip

Regarde attentivement la vidéo de Grayhawk pour t'inspirer de ses **gestes**.

GRAMMAIRE

- Prétérit *BE* + *-ing* → WB p. 123

Language tools

Apprends ces mots avec leur prononciation !

Words

Storytelling

Track 112

- **sto**ry / tale / myth / **le**gend
- pass on / tell
- **he**ro
- a long time a**go**, **sud**denly, /ʌ/ **all** of a **sud**den, then

storyteller

audience = **pub**lic /ɒ:/

animals:

alligator

rabbit

deer /ɪə/

possum /ɑ/

buffalo /ʌ/

moose

ra**coon** /rə'ku:n/

porcupine /'pɔ:kjʊpaɪn/

Places

Track 113

- state (e.g. *Louisiana*)
- **ci**ty (e.g. *New Orleans*)

People

Track 114

- **na**tion = tribe or group of tribes /eɪ/
- **el**ders / **an**cestors
- **house**hold

Grammar

Prétérit simple / Prétérit *Be* + *-ing*

– You **woke** me up! What **were** you **doing**?
– I **was drinking** water.

BE conjugué au Prétérit	Infinitif du verbe + *-ing*

- Ici, l'alligator **rapporte un événement** (le lapin l'a réveillé), puis il **demande des explications sur les circonstances** de cet événement. Le lapin **donne ensuite ces explications**.
- Lorsqu'on évoque un événement passé dans le seul but d'informer, on utilise le **Prétérit simple**. Lorsqu'on souhaite expliquer / justifier les circonstances d'un événement passé, on utilise le **Prétérit *BE* + *-ing***.

(!) *BE* est auxiliaire, c'est donc lui qui :

– prend la marque de la conjugaison (ici, le Prétérit)
– s'accorde avec le sujet *(was/were)*
– permet de construire certaines phrases interrogatives ou négatives *(wasn't / weren't)*

Je prononce

Track 115

La prononciation de *was/were*

a. Écoute les phrases suivantes en faisant attention à la prononciation des mots en gras:

1. *He **was** sleeping when the alarm rang.*
2. *Where **were** you? I **was** at the library*
3. *The alligator **wasn't** happy at all.*
4. *You **weren't** at school, **were** you?*

b. Dans la phrase 2, entends-tu la différence de prononciation entre *where* et *were* ?

c. Entraîne-toi à répéter ces phrases.

Track 150 *Sing, sang, sung* with Fluency MC

Exercices

→ WB p. 121-124

Great reads for TEENS

TOM GATES

Camping Sucks

This year Dad said, "Let's go camping, it's cheap." Mum didn't seem that keen, but I've never been camping before, so I was looking forward to it.

Dad and I went to the camping shop to buy a few essential items like:

"We won't need much," he said.

But the camping shop had some cool stuff and Dad got carried away. He spent a LOT of money and made me promise not to tell Mum.

"We could have stayed in a nice hotel, it would have been cheaper," Dad said.

"Not the same as sleeping under the stars and waking up in the fresh air!" said the man in the shop as he took Dad's money.

On top of everything Dad bought ... Mum packed a whole lot more. The car was stuffed. My sister, Delia, wasn't happy about coming with us. She's not allowed to stay in the house on her own any more, because she had a WILD party the last time Mum and Dad went away. (I stayed next door with Derek. His parents got woken up and weren't happy either.)

We set off, and for a while the holiday was going well. Then we took a wrong turning and got lost.

Mum blamed Dad for not listening to her properly. Dad blamed Mum for not reading the map the right way. They both blamed each other.

It was only when the car got a flat tyre  that they stopped arguing. They phoned the Car Rescue Service, who eventually turned up.

It took AGES to fix the tyre and we didn't make it to the campsite until it was dark. Delia wasn't happy (Delia's never happy). She said the place looked RANK and she couldn't get a signal for her phone. Ha! ha! ha! I thought it looked OK. So I helped Dad with the tent while Mum unpacked the car. (Delia did nothing.)

The tent was tricky to put up, but we did the best we could.

It was a bit late to eat. Dad said, "I'll cook a big breakfast in the morning." But my stomach kept rumbling and I couldn't get to sleep. Then I remembered the secret stash of biscuits in my bag. So I grabbed them and ate them all! Crumbs got everywhere and it was very uncomfortable in my sleeping bag. Even though we had a "family tent" with separate rooms, Delia could hear me shifting around and fidgeting. It was really annoying her. BRILLIANT! So I did it some more. But at the same time I could also hear Mum and Dad ...

SNoring  and that was keeping me awake too. The noise was awful. It seemed to be getting louder and LOUDER. It was almost like thunder, deep and rumbly. Then I realized it sounded like thunder ... because it was thunder. Which was getting closer. There was lightning, too, and really heavy rain that was right above our tent. The storm was HUGE and it didn't take long for the tent to blow away.

Everyone had to run to the car for cover. The storm lasted all night long and everything we had got wet and muddy.  Dad had pitched the tent RIGHT NEXT TO A STREAM! Which flooded and all our stuff got soaked.

Nobody slept at all. It was miserable. 

The Brilliant World of Tom Gates,
Liz Pichon, 2011

Read and explore

- What do you learn about Tom Gates's holidays?

People | *Type of accommodation* | *Problems*

- Did Tom enjoy the holidays? How do you know?

Project

Best holiday ever!

Write a chapter about your funniest holidays!

OR

Draw a doodle of your best holidays and present it to the class.

POEMS

I think my dad is Dracula

I think my dad is Dracula.
I know that sounds insane,
but listen for a moment and
allow me to explain.
We don't live in a castle,
and we never sleep in caves.
But, still, there's something weird
about the way my dad behaves.
I never see him go out
in the daytime when it's light.
He sleeps all day till evening,
then he leaves the house at night.
He comes home in the morning
saying, "Man, I'm really dead!"
He kisses us goodnight, and then
by sunrise he's in bed.
My mom heard my suspicion
and she said, "You're not too swift.
Your father's not a vampire.
He just works the graveyard shift."

Kenn Nesbitt, 2009

Read and explore Track 116

- Why does the boy think his dad is Dracula?
- Listen to the poem, and practice saying it aloud.
- Do you think that someone you know has a secret life?

Project

Write a poem

"I think my (cousin/mum/friend...) is..."
Write a poem about someone you know, using the same style as the poem above. Don't forget the rhymes!

Voodoo girl

Her skin is white cloth,
and she's all sewn apart
and she has many colored pins
sticking out of her heart.

She has a beautiful set
of hypno-disk eyes,
the ones that she uses
to hypnotise guys.

She has many different zombies
who are deeply in her trance.
She even has a zombie
who was originally from France.

But she knows she has a curse on her,
a curse she cannot win.
For if someone gets
too close to her,

the pins stick farther in.

The Melancoly Death of Oyster and Other Stories, Tim Burton, 1997

Read and explore

- Read the poem and try to visualise "the voodoo girl". Then draw her.
- Can you imagine *who she is* *how she feels* ?
- What do you think the poem is about?

Project

Emotions and feelings

Make a figurine that represents your feelings and write a poem about it. You can use this poem as a model.

NOVEL

Miss Peregrine's Home for Peculiar Children

More fantastic still were his stories about life in the Welsh children's home. It was an enchanted place, he said, designed to keep kids safe from the monsters, on an island where the sun shone every day and nobody ever got sick or died. Everyone lived together in a big house that was protected by a wise old bird—or so the story went. As I got older, though, I began to have doubts.

"But why did the monsters want to hurt you?" I asked.
"Because we weren't like other people. We were peculiar."
"Peculiar how?"

"Oh, all sorts of ways, he said. "There was a girl who could fly, a boy who had bees living inside him, a brother and sister who could lift boulders over their heads."

It was hard to tell if he was being serious. Then again, my grandfather was not known as a teller of jokes. He frowned, reading the doubt on my face.

"Fine, you don't have to take my word for it," he said. "I got pictures!" He pushed back his lawn chair and went into the house, leaving me alone on the screened-in lanai. A minute later he came back holding an old cigar box.

I leaned in to look as he drew out four wrinkled and yellowing snapshots.

The first was a blurry picture of what looked like a suit of clothes with no person in them. Either that or the person didn't have a head.

"Sure, he's got a head!" my grandfather said, grinning "Only you can't see it."

"Why not? Is he invisible?"

"Hey, look at the brain on this one!" He raised his eyebrows as if I'd surprised him with my powers of deduction. "Millard, his name was. Funny kid. Sometimes he'd say, 'Hey Abe, I know what you did today,' and he'd tell you where you'd been, what you had to eat, if you picked your nose when you thought nobody was looking. Sometimes he'd follow you, quiet as a mouse, with no clothes on so you couldn't see him—just watching!" He shook his head. "Of all the things, eh?"

He slipped me another photo. Once I'd had a moment to look at it, he said, "So? What do you see?"

"A little girl?"

"And?"

"She's wearing a crown."

He tapped the bottom of the picture. "What about her feet?"

I held the snapshot closer. The girl's feet weren't touching the ground. But she wasn't jumping—she seemed to be floating in the air. My jaw fell open.

"She's flying!"

"Close," my grandfather said." She's levitating. Only she couldn't control herself too well, so sometimes we had to tie a rope around her to keep her from floating away!"

My eyes were glued to her haunting, doll-like face. "Is it real?"

"Of course it is," he said gruffly, taking the picture and replacing it with another, this one of a scrawny boy lifting a boulder. "Victor and his sister weren't so smart, he said, but boy were they strong!"

"He doesn't look strong," I said, studying the boy's skinny arms.

"Trust me, he was. I tried to arm-wrestle him once and he just about tore my hand off!"

But the strangest photo was the last one. It was the back of somebody's head, with a face painted on it.

I stared at the last photo as Grandpa Portman explained. "He had two mouths, see? One in the front and one in the back. That's why he got so big and fat!"

"But it's fake," I said. "The face is just painted on."

"Sure, the paint's fake. It was for a circus show. But I'm telling you, he had two mouths. You don't believe me?"

I thought about it, looking at the pictures and then at my grandfather, his face so earnest and open. What reason would he have to lie?

"I believe you," I said.

Miss Peregrine's Home for Peculiar Children, Ransom Riggs, 2011

Read and explore

- Make as many links as you can between the text and the pictures.
- Who is the narrator of the story? What is peculiar about him?
- Draw a portrait for each character described in the text. Which one do you prefer? Why?

Project

Create a new character for Miss Peregrine's home

Draw it or make a collage, then write a short text about it, starting with: "But the strangest photo was the last one...". Then present your character and its particularities to the class.

ACCOMPAGNEMENT AP PERSONNALISÉ

Get better at...

Get better at...

listening to English

→ Prépare-toi à écouter

On écoute toujours **dans un contexte particulier** : dans la classe, dans un lieu public, chez soi, à la télévision (en fonction de la chaîne que tu sélectionnes, par exemple, tu ne t'attends pas à entendre la même chose), à la radio ou au cinéma... Le contexte peut t'aider à **comprendre le sujet général**.

- **Appuie-toi sur tous les indices que tu peux trouver dans le document ci-dessous pour anticiper le contenu du document sonore correspondant.**

→ Sois actif pendant l'écoute

Lorsque tu écoutes un document sonore, tu comprends toujours quelque chose ! Par exemple, si tu parviens à **identifier différentes voix**, tu peux savoir combien il y a d'interlocuteurs, si ce sont des hommes ou des femmes et parfois même, leur âge.

Ensuite, il faut adapter **tes stratégies**. Tu peux t'appuyer sur :

les sons, puis les mots accentués | *l'intonation* | *les bruits d'ambiance* | *les pauses* | *le ton*

Comment repérer les mots accentués ? Track 117

Ce sont ceux qui contiennent une syllabe sur laquelle la personne qui parle insiste :

- en "appuyant" sur cette syllabe,
- en faisant monter l'intonation avant de redescendre.

À toi de jouer !

- **Écoute le début du document de la page précédente.** Track 118

  Que comprends-tu ? Des mots ? Des sons ?
- **Dans cette phrase, les mots et syllabes en gras sont accentués :**

  "They have **one** very big **thing** in **com**mon." Track 119

  Entends-tu ce phénomène ?
- **Écoute la suite puis explique ce que tu as compris à un(e) camarade.** Track 120

  Aimerais-tu être à la place d'Ema ou d'Alen ?

Fais le bilan → WB p. 134

Complète ta fiche de stratégies.

Game time!

Stand up game

- **Tu vas entendre des instructions. Dès que l'une d'entre elles te concerne, lève-toi !** Track 121
  Exemple : *Stand up if... you have a dog.*
- **À toi de jouer ! Donne des instructions à la classe... Qui va se lever ?**

→ À ton rythme

Dans une situation d'entraînement et de travail en autonomie, tu pourras écouter l'enregistrement plusieurs fois et comme tu le souhaites. Voici **deux façons d'écouter un document** :

1. En entier, plusieurs fois de suite avec une pause entre chaque écoute.
2. Une fois en entier, puis une ou plusieurs fois en discontinu.

→ Laquelle te semblerait la plus efficace ?

À toi de jouer !

- **Tu vas écouter deux documents. Prépare-toi à l'écoute.**

  Regarde les images, à quoi peux-tu t'attendre ?

Track 122

Track 123

- Choisis un mode d'écoute pour chaque document, ou le même pour les deux, comme tu préfères.

  Si tu as testé les deux modes, as-tu l'impression que l'un des deux te convient mieux ?

→ Entraîne ta mémoire immédiate

Lorsque tu écoutes un document sonore en classe, tu es généralement invité(e) à t'en servir tout de suite (pour partager ce que tu as compris avec tes camarades, ou l'expliquer lors d'une évaluation). Pour te rappeler de mieux en mieux ce que tu as entendu, entraîne ta **« mémoire immédiate »** !

À toi de jouer !

- **Écoute des suites de mots.** Track 124
  Essaie de les retenir au fur et à mesure que tu les entends puis dis-les à haute voix.
  Enregistre-toi : as-tu réussi à les citer tous ?
- **Écoute de courts messages audio.** Track 125
  Que parviens-tu à retenir ?

→ Repère les idées

Fais des liens entre les mots accentués que tu as entendus et recrée du sens en faisant appel... à ton bon sens !

À toi de jouer !

- **Tu vas entendre des séries de mots.** Track 126
  Essaie de reconstituer le message dont ils ont été extraits.
  Tu peux dire tes propositions à l'oral ou les écrire sur une feuille.
  Compare avec tes camarades. Avez-vous tous imaginé la même chose ?

Autocorrection Track 126
À la suite de l'activité, tu pourras écouter un corrigé.

→ Un peu de bon sens !

Quelquefois, on peut confondre un mot lors du repérage. Il faut donc **retrouver la bonne information** grâce au contexte.

À toi de jouer !

- **Écoute ce document.** Track 127
  Un élève peut avoir repéré les mots suivants :

  Harry – 12 – wizard – magic want

  Il peut comprendre alors qu'on parle de Harry Potter. Mais à quoi correspondrait *want* ? Réfléchis, puis écoute le Coup de pouce.
- **Écoute des suites de mots isolés.** Track 129
  Quel message pourrais-tu restituer pour chacune de ces suites ?
  Ce message te semble-t-il logique ? As-tu réussi à déduire le sens des mots que tu ne connaissais pas ?
- Un mot ne convient pas pour reconstituer l'un des messages logiquement. Trouve-le puis justifie ton choix.

Coup de pouce Tracks 128-130
Si tu en as besoin, écoute des aides à l'issue des deux activités.

Game time!

Guess the picture

• **Pour chaque série, trouve l'image dont parle la personne que tu vas entendre.** Track 131

1

a.

b.

c.

2

a.

b.

c.

3

a.

b.

c.

4

a.

b.

c.

5

a.

b.

c.

6

a.

b.

c.

Get better at...

speaking English

→ Pour bien parler, il faut se lancer !

Prends l'habitude d'**écouter régulièrement de l'anglais** pour pouvoir ensuite **imiter ce que tu entends.** Commence par des phrases courtes, en faisant attention à **la mélodie de la phrase** (l'intonation), à **l'accentuation** des syllabes dans les mots, et des mots dans la phrase.

À toi de jouer !

- **Tu vas entendre des phrases en anglais.** Track 132

  Écoute-les attentivement puis répète-les en essayant d'imiter l'intonation et la prononciation.
- **Enregistre-toi** (sur un site comme www.vocaroo.com ou sur un téléphone) puis compare avec le modèle. Tu peux recommencer jusqu'à ce que tu sois satisfait(e) !

→ Un peu de clarté

Quand tu te prépares à parler en anglais, commence par **bien lire le sujet** pour le comprendre. **Ensuite rassemble tes idées... en anglais bien sûr !** Mobilise tes connaissances et essaie d'**organiser** ce que tu veux dire.

- **Voici trois sujets que tu pourrais avoir à traiter.**

  → Lis-les en t'assurant que tu les comprends bien.

Make the class guess the name of a famous person

Make the class guess what your favourite English food is

Present a monument to the class

- **En haut de la page 127 tu vas trouver des notes que l'on pourrait prendre pour traiter l'un de ces trois sujets.**

  → Lis-les : peux-tu deviner de quel sujet elles traitent ? Et même, de qui/de quoi on parle précisément ?

Ce que je veux communiquer

Idées
Physical description
Personality
People's feelings
His job

Informations culturelles
first black President
elected twice → 2x4 years
Democrat

De quelles connaissances ai-je besoin ?

Vocabulaire
tall
married
2 daughters
cheerful
popular
worked for 8 years
in Washington D.C
first black President

Grammaire
Be
Have
Present
Preterit
superlative

Suis-je certain(e) de la **prononciation** des mots que je vais employer ?

À toi de jouer !

- **Tu as deviné ? Alors utilise les notes ci-dessus pour t'entraîner.**
  Enregistre-toi et écoute-toi.
- **À ton tour !**

→ Choisis l'un des trois sujets proposés p. 126
→ Décide de quoi/de qui tu vas parler
→ Réfléchis à ce que tu vas dire et développe ton sujet
→ Puis fais ta présentation orale !

Autocorrection Track 133
Écoute une production possible à partir de ces notes.

Game time!

Serial talkers

- **Écoute des séries de mots et complète-les logiquement.** Track 134
  Ex. : *a schoolbag, a textbook, a pencil case...*
- **À ton tour :** propose un mot à un(e) camarade qui doit alors t'en proposer un autre, lié thématiquement. Continuez jusqu'à ce que l'un de vous n'ait plus rien à dire !

→ Tu peux quand même le dire...

S'il te manque un mot, ne t'inquiète pas : tu peux très bien t'en sortir ! il suffit de le **dire autrement**... Imagine par exemple qu'il te manque le mot "*bear*" (ours) :

Technique n°1 – **donne une définition**
She was attacked by ***a big animal. It is usually dangerous and lives in the mountains.***

OU

Technique n°2 – **utilise un terme plus large**
She was attacked by ***a big brown animal.***

OU

Technique n°3 – **utilise un terme plus précis**
She was attacked by ***a grizzly.***

À toi de jouer !

- **Tu vas écouter deux phrases définissant un mot.** Track 135
  Dis ce mot à voix haute dès que tu l'as trouvé !
- **À ton tour ! Choisis un mot dans ton manuel et fais-le deviner à un(e) camarade.**

Autocorrection Track 135
À la suite de l'activité, tu pourras écouter un corrigé.

→ Ne t'arrête pas !

Quand tu t'exprimes, **la fluidité de ton discours** est importante pour que l'on comprenne facilement ce que tu veux dire. Assurer **les liaisons** entre les mots y contribue grandement.

- **Écoute cette phrase en faisant attention aux éléments indiqués :**

  She is really interested in astronomy. Track 136

- Répète cette phrase en imitant la manière dont elle est dite et en tenant compte des liaisons.

Les règles d'or des liaisons !

- Quand deux sons consonnes identiques se suivent, on ne les répète pas. On ne prononce que le 2e de ces sons, qui se trouve au début du 2e mot.
- Quand un son consonne est suivi d'un son voyelle, on fait la liaison entre les deux sons. Track 137

I take care of my brother.
He hates Sundays.
Boston is an interesting place.
I am not involved anymore.

À toi de jouer !

- **De la bouche à l'oreille...**
  Choisis une phrase ci-dessous et dis-la à un(e) camarade dans le creux de l'oreille ; il/elle la transmettra à son tour à un(e) autre camarade... Les liaisons seront-elles toutes respectées à l'arrivée ?

Never accept an apple.
Toby's aunt is an incredible artist.
It's easy as 1-2-3!
My parents are impossible!
Margaret is an amazing inspector.
It isn't expensive at all!

Autocorrection Track 138
À la fin de l'activité, écoutez les phrases enregistrées pour vous corriger.

→ L'intonation exprime tes intentions

L'intonation en anglais **monte ou descend**. Cela dépend du type de phrases (interrogative, déclarative...) mais aussi **des intentions** de celui qui parle.

- **Écoute ces phrases.** Track 139
  1. Do you like classical music?
  2. Where did you buy this book?
  3. You work at the science museum, don't you?
  4. She looked everywhere in the living-room, the kitchen, the bathroom and the bedroom.
  5. One of my favourite pastimes is watching movies, especially when it's cold outside and you can snuggle under a duvet with a cup of cocoa.
  6. You're enjoying this, aren't you?

→ Pour chacune : l'intonation est-elle montante ou descendante ? Sur quel mot ?

→ Lorsque l'intonation n'est pas celle que l'on pourrait attendre, quel est l'effet obtenu ?

Autocorrection Track 139
À la suite de l'activité, tu pourras écouter un corrigé.

À toi de jouer !

- **Demande à ton voisin/ta voisine de choisir un nombre de 1 à 6.**
Lis la phrase correspondante avec l'intonation qui convient :

1. This is my sister Anna.	4. Which painting do you like best?
2. Do you know Ethan?	5. He came in and I ignored him.
3. My favourite fruits are bananas, apples and kiwis.	6. This book is wonderful!

Autocorrection Track 140
À la suite de l'activité, tu pourras écouter un corrigé.

- **Écoute des phrases. Grâce à l'intonation, repère le contexte dans lequel chacune a été dite :**

lors d'une conférence | *dans un lieu public* | *au cinéma* | *dans la rue* — Track 141

- **Répète-les le plus fidèlement possible.**
Enregistre-toi puis compare avec le modèle.

Fais le bilan → WB p. 136
Complète ta fiche de stratégies.

→ Ça ne manque pas de rythme !

- **Dans les mots suivants, les lettres muettes sont barrées :**

fantastic~~a~~lly – choc~~o~~late – logic~~a~~lly – comf~~o~~rtable – veg~~e~~table – bus~~i~~ness

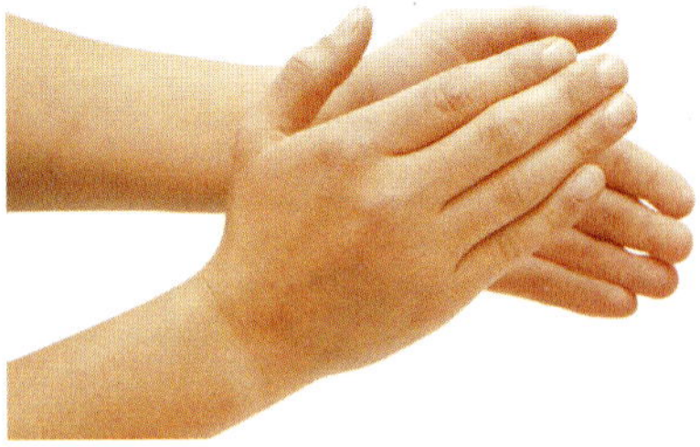

- **Écoute ces mots et frappe dans tes mains pour marquer chaque syllabe.** Track 142

Game time!

Le labyrinthe des lettres muettes

- **Sors du labyrinthe en traçant le chemin avec ton doigt.**

Pour avancer, trouve les mots comportant des lettres muettes.
Attention, tu n'as pas le droit d'aller en diagonale !

Coup de pouce Track 143
Tu peux écouter ces mots pour t'aider à avancer !

start →

cam~~e~~ra	line	famous	midnight	monument
int~~e~~resting	temperature	hot	painting	polite
decide	restaurant	laboratory	muscle	classmate
little	eyes	situation	vegetable	listen
yellow	dress	conclusion	teacher	could

→ end

Utilise le site English Central

Cet excellent site propose des activités d'écoute, de mémorisation de vocabulaire mais surtout d'entraînement à l'expression orale.

- On y trouve un grand nombre de vidéos de toutes sortes, notamment pour les jeunes apprenants.
- Tu pourras visionner, écouter et répéter le contenu des vidéos de ton choix, puis le site évaluera ta performance et te donnera des conseils.

N'hésite pas à t'en servir avec tes parents !
www.englishcentral.com

EnglishCentral
Learn English with the World's Best Videos

Videos | Courses

TOPICS

> All
> Academic English
> Business English
> Media English
> Social English
> Travel English
> Young Learners

Get better at...

reading in English

→ Anticipe et crée des liens

Lorsque tu lis en anglais, tu rencontres des mots que tu connais mais aussi beaucoup de **mots nouveaux**. Pas de panique : certaines **stratégies** te permettront d'apprendre à te débrouiller !

- **Avant de commencer la lecture, observe les informations autour du texte :**

titre | *auteur* | *illustrations* | ...

Elles peuvent t'aider à anticiper le contenu du texte.

→ Les illustrations : que vois-tu ? Imagine ce qui s'est passé.

→ Lis le titre et essaie de faire des liens avec l'illustration.

It was 7 minutes after midnight. The dog was lying on the grass in the middle of the lawn in front of Mrs Shears' house. Its eyes were closed. It looked as if it was running on its side, the way dogs run when they think they are chasing a cat in a dream. But the dog was not running or asleep. The dog was dead. There was a garden fork sticking out of the dog. [...] I went through Mrs Shears' gate, closing it behind me. I walked onto her lawn and knelt beside the dog. I put my hand on the muzzle of the dog. It was still warm.

The Curious Incident of the Dog In The Night-Time, Mark Haddon, 2004

- **Maintenant lis le texte.**

→ Rencontres-tu certains mots auxquels tu t'attendais ?

→ Y en a-t-il un qui te semble particulièrement important ?

- Relis le texte en te concentrant sur les occurrences du mot *dog* : qu'apprends-tu à chaque fois qu'il est mentionné ?

- **Repère :**

les personnages

recherche :

- **les mots commençant par une majuscule**. (S'agit-il bien de personnes ?)
- **les pronoms personnels**. (Tu peux commencer par *I*, *she*, *he* et *it*. À qui/quoi font-ils référence ?)

les lieux

recherche :

- **les mots commençant par une majuscule**. (S'agit-il bien de lieux ?)
- **les prépositions de lieux :** *in*, *on*, *to*, *in front of*, *behind*, *beside*...

le temps

recherche :

- **les jours, les heures, les années...**
- **les prépositions de temps :** *at*, *in*, *on*, *during*, *before*...

- Quelles autres informations as-tu apprises ? Si nécessaire, compare avec un camarade.
- Que peux-tu t'imaginer grâce à la dernière phrase ? Écris quelques phrases pour continuer ce texte.

À toi de jouer !

- **Observe cette couverture de livre.**
  Lis les trois résumés et devine quel est celui qui correspond au livre :

1. Starting middle school brings all the usual challenges – until the unthinkable happens, and Fern and her family must find a way to heal. Twelve-year-old Fern feels invisible.
   ▾ Read more

2. Ollie and Moritz are best friends, but they can never meet. Ollie has a life-threatening allergy to electricity, and Moritz's weak heart requires a pacemaker. If they ever did meet, they could both die. ▾ Read more

3. It happens every year before homecoming – the list is posted all over school. Two girls are picked from each grade. One is named the prettiest, one the ugliest.
   ▾ Read more

→ Quels indices t'ont permis de deviner ?

- **Choisis un autre résumé parmi les deux autres et dessine la couverture qui pourrait l'illustrer.**

→ Comprendre sans tout savoir

Tu n'as pas besoin de connaitre chaque mot pour réussir à **comprendre l'essentiel d'un texte**.

- Fais-en l'expérience en lisant cet extrait de *Tom Gates*. Certains mots moins connus ont été effacés.

Pour essayer de deviner le sens de ces mots il faudra :
– t'appuyer sur le contexte immédiat pour inférer ce qu'ils pourraient signifier,
– comprendre la fonction de ces mots dans la phrase.

Tu peux pour cela t'appuyer sur :
→ les illustrations ❶
→ les mots transparents ❷
→ les mots dont la racine et la composition peuvent faire deviner le sens ❸
→ les majuscules ❹
→ les prépositions (pour repérer les lieux, le temps...) ❺

It was only when the car got a flat tyre that they stopped arguing. They phoned the Car Rescue Service, who eventually [redacted]

It took AGES to fix the tyre and we didn't [redacted] to the campsite until it was dark. Delia wasn't happy (Delia's never happy). She said the place looked [redacted] and she couldn't get a signal for her phone. Ha! ha! ha! I thought it looked OK. So I helped Dad with the tent [redacted] Mum unpacked the car. (Delia did nothing.)

The Brilliant World of Tom Gates, Liz Pichon, 2011

- **Visualise la série d'événements. Et si tu ajoutais d'autres dessins ?**

Inférer les mots inconnus

Si certains mots te sont inconnus, tu peux parfois **deviner leur sens** grâce à différents indices. C'est un peu comme mener une enquête !

- **Un des mots cachés a été révélé !** Relis la phrase pour trouver les indices qui t'aideront à en trouver le sens.

Delia est associée à des formes négatives !

"Rank" donne une information sur l'apparence du lieu. Penses-tu que Delia a un avis positif sur le camping ? Et pourquoi ce mot est-il écrit en majuscules ?

"Delia wasn't happy. (Delia's never happy.) She said the place **looked** RANK and she couldn't get a signal for her phone."

and est un connecteur logique. Il permet d'ajouter une information nouvelle qui renforce une information existante.

Coup de pouce Track 144

Comment inférer le sens des mots inconnus ? En t'appuyant sur :
- la structure de la phrase,
- la formation des mots,
- leur ressemblance avec le français,
- les connecteurs logiques.

À toi de jouer !

- **Essaie de deviner approximativement le sens des mots qui te sont inconnus :**

1. My sister bought a white t-shirt, black boots and a black dungarees!
2. Amy likes jazz, rock and roll, rap and dubstep.
3. I got delayed on my way to school, so I ran.
4. We love watching movies, reading books but we hate playing chess.
5. He ate an apple, an orange and longans.

Fais le bilan → WB p. 138

Complète ta fiche de stratégies.

Game time!

Read, visualize and draw

Her name is Ophelia. She is short and has one side of her hair curly and the other side straight. She has tan-colored skin and likes to walk in the rain. She has gray-colored eyes and she likes to wear lavender dresses.

Get better at...

writing in English

→ K.I.S.S. (Keep it short and simple!)

Pour écrire en anglais, ne cède pas à la tentation de passer par le français. Tu as bien plus de connaissances que tu ne l'imagines : **fais-toi confiance... et lis ton sujet avec attention,** cela te donnera forcément des idées ! Pour commencer, tu peux **rédiger des phrases simples.**

- **Observe les premières lignes de ce livre intitulé *The Lost Diary of Snow White* :**

> This diary is the property of Snow White. Strictly speaking, I am not supposed to keep a diary. No fairytale characters are. It's the unwritten rule of the land.
>
> Boyd Brent, *The Lost Diary of Snow White*, 1988

- Comme tu le vois, ce sont des phrases courtes qui suivent presque toutes une structure simple :

Sujet + Verbe + Complément

À toi de jouer !

- **Voici des éléments, fais des phrases en piochant dans chaque liste** (si tu as besoin d'aide, relis l'histoire de ces personnages dans ton manuel, p. 42-43) :

Tom Gates Delia Derek	loves is has	a sister. always late. unhappy. annoying. a very good friend. a pair of sunglasses.

→ Enrichis et varie le lexique

Lorsque tu te prépares à écrire, essaie de mobiliser **un vocabulaire précis et varié.**
Pour cela, sois attentif aux mots que tu rencontres quand tu lis en anglais : observe la manière dont ils sont employés, note-les dans ton cahier ou dans un petit carnet, et joue avec !

À toi de jouer !

- **Sur les deux pages suivantes tu vas trouver des activités proposées aux jeunes anglophones, notamment pour faire du *creative writing*.**
- **Lis le document de la page 136, observe chaque catégorie d'adjectifs, vérifie le sens de ceux qui sont nouveaux pour toi puis utilise-les dans des phrases.**

- **Complète chacune de ces cinq listes avec les adjectifs suivants :**

impressive, beautiful, microscopic, exciting, scary, graceful, old, charming, adorable...

Enrichis ces listes tout au long de l'année... et même, tout au long du collège !

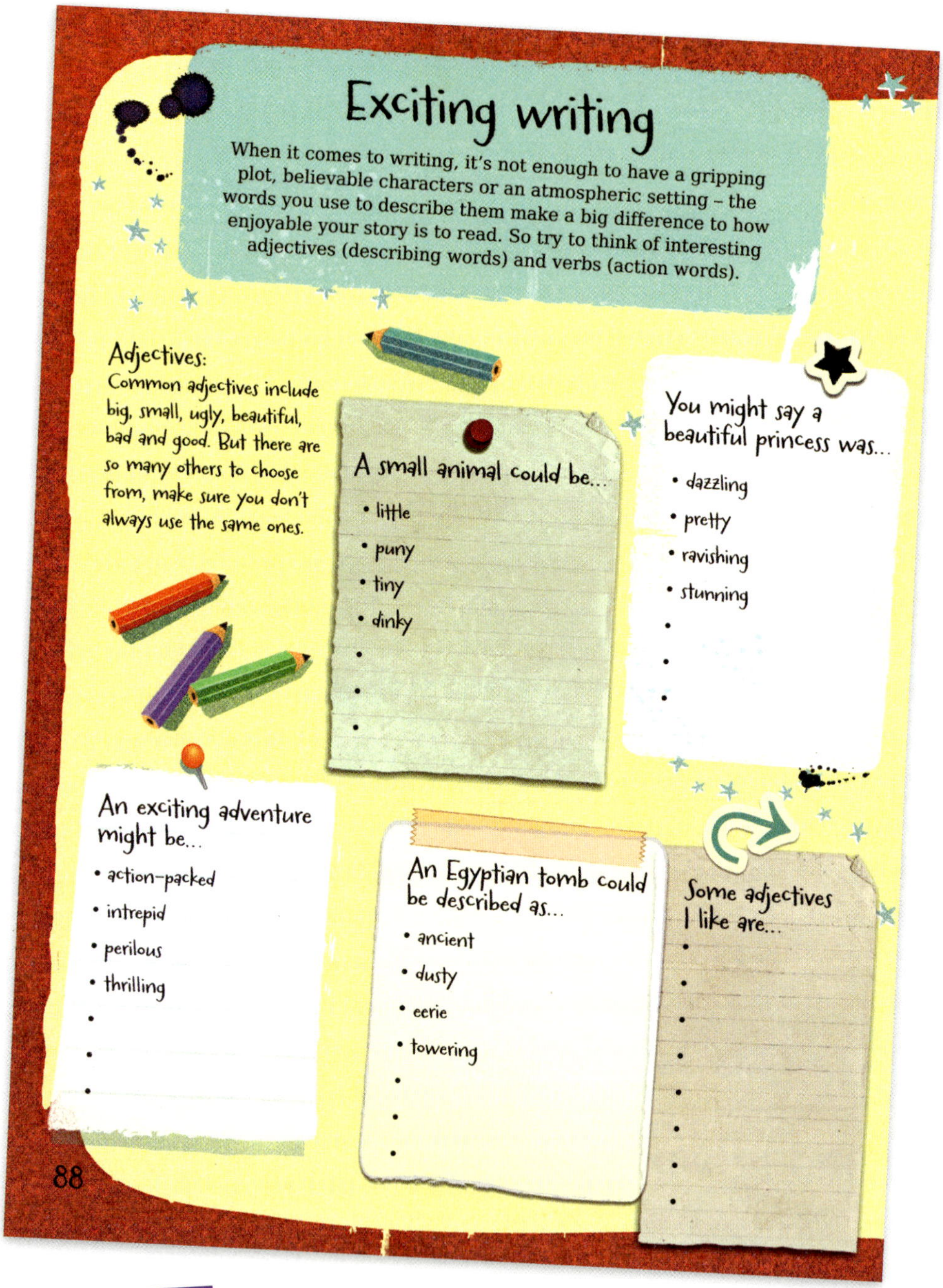

Exciting writing

When it comes to writing, it's not enough to have a gripping plot, believable characters or an atmospheric setting – the words you use to describe them make a big difference to how enjoyable your story is to read. So try to think of interesting adjectives (describing words) and verbs (action words).

Adjectives:
Common adjectives include big, small, ugly, beautiful, bad and good. But there are so many others to choose from, make sure you don't always use the same ones.

A small animal could be...
- little
- puny
- tiny
- dinky
-
-
-

You might say a beautiful princess was...
- dazzling
- pretty
- ravishing
- stunning
-
-
-

An exciting adventure might be...
- action-packed
- intrepid
- perilous
- thrilling
-
-
-

An Egyptian tomb could be described as...
- ancient
- dusty
- eerie
- towering
-
-
-

Some adjectives I like are...
-
-
-
-
-
-
-
-

88

Game time!

L'hyperphrase

Utilise un adjectif de chacune des listes ci-dessus dans une seule et même phrase. Puis, fais la même chose avec les verbes de la page 137.

Trouvez l'intrus

Fais une phrase dans laquelle tu glisses un adjectif ou un verbe incongru... Tes camarades s'en rendront-ils compte ?

- **Maintenant, joue avec les verbes ! Observe les trois listes ci-dessous, vérifie le sens des verbes qui sont nouveaux pour toi, puis utilise-les pour créer des phrases.**

Verbs:
These tell you what a character or thing does, thinks or feels and can reflect a person's mood or personality.

When I'm in a hurry, I...
- rush
- panic
- speed
- sprint
-
-
-

When I'm with my friends, I...
- laugh
- joke
- play
- chatter
-
-
-

When I'm angry, I...
- shout
- sulk
- stamp
- scowl
-
-
-

- **Complète chacune de ces trois listes avec les verbes suivants :**

go to the cinema, run, chat, slam my bedroom door, feel comfortable...

Enrichis ces listes tout au long de l'année... et même, tout au long du collège !

À toi de jouer !

- **Complète ces trois débuts de phrases comme tu le souhaites :**

Écoute, écris, relis

Pour **écrire correctement** en anglais et **te relire efficacement**, commence par t'entraîner avec de courtes dictées. Tu seras plus attentif à :

l'orthographe des mots > la ponctuation des phrases > l'ordre des mots dans la phrase

À toi de jouer !

Step 1 **Écoute une série de mots et écris-les.** Track 145

→ Essaie de te rappeler le contexte dans lequel tu as déjà vu ces mots puis essaie de les visualiser pour bien les écrire.

Autocorrection Track 145
À la suite de l'activité, tu pourras écouter un corrigé.

- **Prononce ces mots après les avoir écrits.** L'orthographe que tu as choisie te semble-t-elle la bonne ?
- **Écoute l'autocorrection et vérifie ton orthographe.**

Step 2 **Un peu plus ambitieux :** procède de la même manière avec des phrases ! Track 146

Coup de pouce
Demande à ton professeur une correction écrite de la dictée.

Ponctue pour être clair

La ponctuation est importante : si elle est mal placée, elle peut conduire à des contre-sens. Pense à la vérifier quand tu relis ce que tu as écrit.

- **Observe ces phrases et compare-les : veulent-elles dire la même chose ?** Vérifie le sens des mots dans un dictionnaire si nécessaire.

Let's eat children! / Let's eat, children!
I am interested in cooking my family and my dog. / I am interested in cooking, my family and my dog.
A panda eats shoots and leaves. / A panda eats, shoots and leaves.

Fais le bilan → WB p. 140

Complète ta fiche de stratégies.

Game time!

Whaaat?

- **La ponctuation, les espaces et les majuscules ont disparu des phrases suivantes !**

→ Rétablis-les, puis essaie de résoudre les énigmes.

Coup de pouce Track 147
Écoute un enregistrement de ces phrases, cela t'aidera à comprendre leur construction.

1. heloveschocolatebutheistoopoortobuysomeeverydaysohehasachocolatebarforhisbirthdayeveryyear
2. Itisabiggreenanimalwhichlivesinriversitisverydangerousbecauseithasreallybigteethitlookslikeaprehistoricanimal
3. theviewfromthismonumentwhichistotallymadeofironisfantasticbecauseyoucanseethewholecapitalcityitsnamestartswithane

90 exercices pour s'entraîner en grammaire

Grammaire
Exercices d'entraînement

Be et *Have*

Be

Besoin d'aide ?
Relis la leçon p. 22.

1 Rédige la présentation d'un nouveau robot pour le magazine de sciences de ton établissement :

age – name – country – city – personality – emotions

2 Complète ces phrases avec la forme appropriée de *Be*.

a. People say that I ... very tall.

b. They ... very nice, they're always criticizing other people.

c. You ... in a good mood. Is it because you had a bad mark this morning?

d. We ... very pleased to meet you!

e. ... they brother and sister?

There is / There are

3 Fais l'inventaire de ce magasin de jouets. Ajoute des jouets supplémentaires. Ton camarade saura-t-il repérer les intrus dans ton inventaire ?

4 Fais 5 phrases pour décrire ce qu'il y a ou non dans ta chambre. Piège tes camarades en ajoutant un mensonge.

Have

Besoin d'aide ?
Relis la leçon p. 22.

5 Choisis un personnage ci-dessous. Rédige quelques lignes pour le décrire. Ton voisin saura-t-il retrouver de qui il s'agit ?

6 Que disent ces personnes ? Complète les bulles en conjuguant correctement *have*.

a.
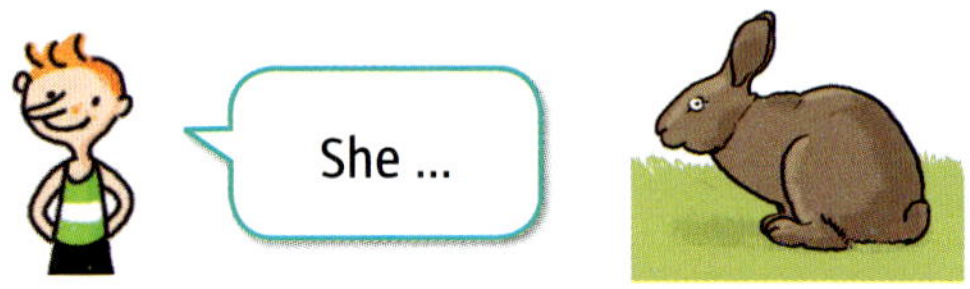

b.

c.
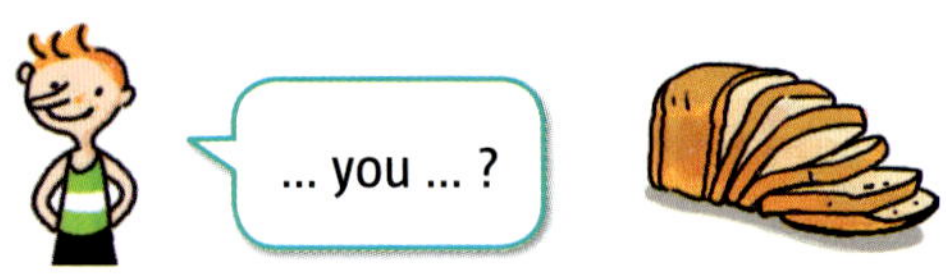

d.

e.

Le choix entre *Be* et *Have*

Besoin d'aide ? Relis la leçon p. 22.

7 ***Be* ou *Have* ?**

This ... Kurt. He ... a teenager. He ... an only child. He ... any brothers or sisters but he ... many friends. He ... tall and he ... blue eyes.

His parents ... quite young: his mother ... 36 and his father ... 40. They ... a big house.

8 Utilise *Be* et *Have* pour décrire ces personnes physiquement.

Le choix de la conjugaison

Présent simple

Besoin d'aide ? Relis les leçons p. 22 et 54.

9 Remets les mots dans le bon ordre pour former des phrases correctes. Attention à la ponctuation !

a. comes / she / Kingdom / the / United / from.

b. on / school / always / they / to / foot / go.

c. favourite / is / pop / your / who / star ?

d. you / who / do / with / live/ ?

e. because / don't / everyday / not / to / they / do sports / they / time / have.

10 Écris un mail à ton correspondant pour te présenter. N'hésite pas à lui poser des questions pour apprendre à le connaître.

11 Conjugue les verbes entre parenthèses au Présent simple.

a. The bakery ... *(close)* at 7:00 p.m.

b. They ... *(not/like)* red meat.

c. I always ... *(take)* the bus to go to school.

d. ... you ... *(like)* pizza?

e. She ... *(not/live)* in Paris, she ... *(live)* in London.

f. We ... *(not/wake up)* at 6:00 in the morning, we ... *(wake up)* at 7:00.

Présent en *Be + -ing*

Besoin d'aide ? Relis la leçon p. 68.

12 Conjugue les verbes entre parenthèses au Présent *Be+ -ing*.

a. I ... *(do)* my homework now because tomorrow I have football practice.

b. "Where ... you ... *(go)* at this time?"
"I ... *(go)* to the cinema because there is a great film I want to see!"

c. Lucy ... *(look)* for her cat, he is not in the house.

d. She ... *(not/watch)* TV because she has a lot of homework to do!

e. We ... *(have)* a great time in London!

13 Décris cette image à ton voisin sans la lui montrer. Explique-lui ce que fait chacun des personnages – il devra les dessiner. Comparez les deux images !

Prétérit simple

Besoin d'aide ?
Relis la leçon p. 36.

14 Challenge : essaie de donner le Prétérit de 10 verbes. Utilise ensuite 3 de ces verbes dans des phrases.

e. g. *come – came*

15 Tu reviens juste de Londres ! Raconte ton voyage.

My parents and I ... *(go)* to London and we ... *(visit)* many famous monuments. Buckingham Palace ... *(be)* my favourite because it is so huge! We also ... *(go)* shopping. My parents ... *(buy)* me a great "I ❤ London" T-shirt. We ... *(have)* so much fun! I ... *(not/want)* to leave London.

16 Voici des inventeurs dont les créations ont changé notre vie quotidienne. Reconstitue les phrases pour les présenter.

a. Dr Martin Cooper / create / the first mobile phone / in 1973

b. Alan Kay / imagine /a "personal, portable information manipulator" / in 1968

c. Percy Spencer / invent / the microwave / in 1945

d. George Beauchamp / design / the first electrically amplified guitar / in 1931

17 Paroles sans images ! Crée 6 vignettes pour illustrer cette histoire.

Arthur was sleeping soundly in his bed when suddenly, his alarm clock went off.

He opened his eyes and turned it off.

Then he rolled out of bed, feeling very tired.

He opened the curtains and noticed that is was still dark...

So he looked up at the big clock in the corridor and saw that it was only 5 a.m.!

He thought: "the alarm clock went on too soon!"

18 Histoire sans paroles ! Raconte ce qui s'est passé.

19 Les parents de Peter lui ont laissé le mot suivant :

Hi sweetheart,

Can you:

- make your bed
- tidy your bedroom
- wash the breakfast dishes
- set the table
- prepare dinner, please?

Thank you so much for your help.
Your dad and I have so much work to do today!

Love you. Mum (and dad).

Peter ne sera pas là à leur retour et leur laisse ce petit mot. Complète-le !

Mum and dad,

I did my best but couldn't do everything because I have to go and work with Jamie!

I ... my bed and I ... my bedroom. I also ... the breakfast dishes. And I ... the table too. Sorry, but I ... dinner. I ... time.

We'll have to order pizzas I am afraid! ☺

Love you more!

Peter

L'utilisation de *Ago*

20 Reformule ces phrases en utilisant *Ago*.

a. Mark graduated in 2012. He is now a famous architect.

b. Sofia got married in 2015 and she had a baby in February 2017.

c. I went to the cinema last Saturday. We saw a great movie!

d. We visited New York in December 2011 but it's so different during the summer that we're hoping to go back soon.

21 Réponds aux questions suivantes avec les informations te concernant. Donne des précisions.

a. How long ago did you start going to school?

b. How long ago did you last go to the restaurant?

c. How long ago did you last go on holidays?

d. How long ago did you last go on a school trip?

Prétérit en *Be + -ing*

Besoin d'aide ?
Relis la leçon p. 108.

22 Choisis entre *was / were / wasn't / weren't*.

a. No, mummy, I ... playing video games, I ... doing my homework!

b. Alex and Jenny ... in the garden when the postman came, they ... gardening.

c. We ... at his party last week, we ... in London.

d. He ... very nice when he was a child, he ... always arguing with his sister.

Le choix entre Prétérit simple et Prétérit *Be + -ing*

Besoin d'aide ?
Relis la leçon p. 108.

23 Conjugue les verbes entre parenthèses. Choisis entre le Prétérit simple et le Prétérit *Be + -ing*.

a. The phone ... *(ring)* just as we ... *(leave)*.

b. I ... *(sleep)* when they ... *(arrive)*.

c. Santa Claus ... *(come in)* while they ... *(sleep)*.

d. He ... *(run)* when he ... *(lose)* his keys.

e. She ... *(do)* her homework when her mother ... *(come)* back home.

24 Utilise le Prétérit et le Prétérit *Be + -ing* pour décrire la situation et expliquer ce qui s'est passé.

a.
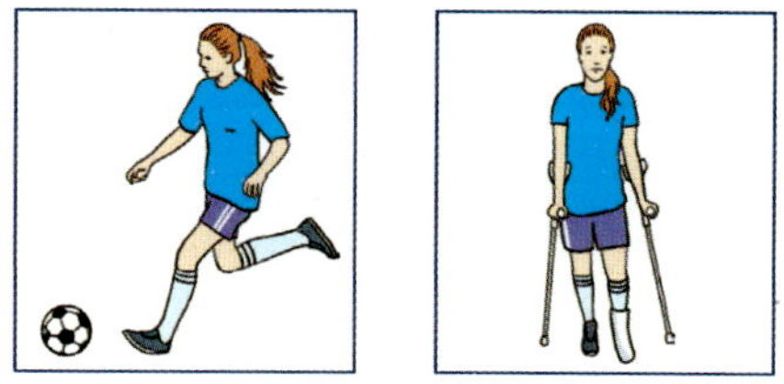

b.

c.

d.

Le choix des modaux

Can

25 Enquête dans la classe. Pose des questions à tes camarades et sois le premier à trouver les talents suivants :

a. Quelqu'un qui sait jouer de la musique.

b. Quelqu'un qui sait monter à cheval.

c. Quelqu'un qui parle plus d'une langue.

d. Quelqu'un qui peut réciter l'alphabet en anglais en partant de la fin !

26 Quelles possibilités t'offrent ces lieux (quand peut-on s'y rendre ? Que peut-on y faire ? etc.) ? Explique à partir des panneaux.

a. 

b. 

c. 

d. 

e. 

f. 

Be able to

27 Tu vas faire un tour au salon de l'invention. Que de choses révolutionnaires ! Que vont-elles nous permettre de faire ? Quelles limites y vois-tu ?

a. The flying shoes:

b. The interactive computer:

c. The homework pen:

d. The feeding pill:

e. The X-Ray glasses:

28 À ton avis, que pourrons-nous faire en 2050 que nous ne pouvons pas encore faire aujourd'hui ? Trouve au moins 5 idées.

Must

29 Fais des phrases pour exprimer les devoirs des superhéros !

30 Les parents de Tom partent en weekend mais ils le contraignent à suivre tout un programme en leur absence. Rédige le message qu'ils lui ont laissé sur la table.

Get up early

Do your homework

Not watch too much TV

Tidy your room

Do the cleaning

Should

31 Donne des conseils à ces personnes :

a. I'm sad. →

b. I have a headache. →

c. I am not very good at English. →

d. Peter and Anna are lost in Dallas. →

e. Laura loves walking but she lives in a city. →

32 Écoute des personnes te faire part de leur problème puis complète chaque phrase avec *should* ou *shouldn't*. Track 148

a. You ... play basketball today.

b. You ... go to the hospital.

c. You ... tell the teacher. He'll understand.

d. You ... spend so much time on screens. Maybe you need to wear glasses!

e. You ... wear these sneakers. You ... wear proper hiking shoes. And you ... take a warmer jacket too!

Will

Besoin d'aide ?
Relis la leçon p. 100.

33 Raconte tout ce que tu feras au collège demain.

34 Que feras-tu dans ces circonstances ?

a. If I earn a lot of money, I ...

b. If I come early to the party, I ...

c. If I go to London, I ...

d. If I meet my favourite actor in the street, I ...

35 Tu as le pouvoir de prédire l'avenir ! Prédis celui des personnes suivantes :

your dad – your mum – your brother – your sister – your best friend

→ You ...

36 Tu veux faire l'acquisition d'un robot. Pose des questions au vendeur.

be my friend – help me do my homework – come to school with me – when / do the shopping – where / sleep

37 Écris 5 messages pour des *Fortune cookies*.

e. g. *You will soon be sitting on top of the world!*

Parler de l'avenir

Les différents choix possibles

Besoin d'aide ?
Relis la leçon p. 100.

38 Tu vas intervenir en tant que roboticien à la convention des robots. Complète ton discours !

« Ladies and gentlemen,

I am so happy to be here to talk about robots because they are amazing.

In the future, robots ... *(be)* everywhere, ladies and gentlemen. They ... *(help)* children at school, they ... *(assist)* us in our work place, they ... *(take care)* of old people in hospitals or retirement homes. We ... *(not/live)* alone in our homes, we ... *(not/have)* to worry anymore. »

39 Remets les éléments dans l'ordre pour former des phrases qui pourraient suivre logiquement celles proposées :

a. Put on your coat!
are / a / you / cold / catch / to / going.

b. Look at the sky!
it / going / is / rain / to.

c. They don't work enough.
to / they / have / going / not / grades / good / are.

d. Liz is in London!
her / are / see / to / going / you / ?

e. My phone is broken.
I / to / one / am / new / buy / a / going.

f. He is nominated as most promising actor.
he / great / actor / going / a / is / be / to ?

40 **Complète ces phrases. Utilise *be going to* pour faire des prédictions :**

e. g. *I'm late*
→ *I'm late, I'm going to miss my train.*

a. Don't jump on the bed! ...

b. Don't eat too much chocolate! ...

c. You shouldn't drive so fast, ...

d. It's really cloudy, ...

e. I haven't revised my lessons, ...

41 **Utilise *be going to* pour conjuguer le verbe entre parenthèses.**

a. We ... *(not/see)* my brother next week, he is in Paris.

b. I ... *(revise)* my lessons this weekend, we have a test on Monday.

c. I don't want to play video games, I ... *(read)* instead.

d. My brother ... *(not/watch)* this film, he hates horror films.

e. You ... *(become)* a great singer, your voice is so beautiful.

f. John and Peter ... *(not/come)*, their car is broken.

Le choix du type d'énoncé

Les énoncés interrogatifs

Besoin d'aide ?
Relis la leçon p. 22, 36 et 82.

42 **Quelles questions ont pu être posées pour obtenir ces réponses ?**

a. Paul

b. In Liverpool.

c. England.

d. One brother and one sister.

e. 13.

f. The Rolling Stones.

43 **Pose des questions à ton camarade pour savoir :**

a. qui est sa star préférée ;

b. s'il a des frères et sœurs, et leur prénom ;

c. quelle est sa matière préférée ;

d. s'il pratique un sport, et lequel ;

e. où il a passé ses dernières vacances.

44 **Remets ces mots dans le bon ordre pour former des phrases interrogatives.**

a. get / email / ? / you / did / my

b. lunch / are / having / for / ? / what /you

c. humans / robots / are / efficient / ? / more / than

d. ? / the / come / you / to / Halloween /will /party

e. your / you / friend's / next / ? / live / to / house / do

f. Indian tribes / were / how many / there / in / America / ?

Les énoncés à l'impératif

45 **Quelles seraient tes 7 recommandations aux enfants pour être en bonne santé ?**

1. ...

2. ...

3. ...

4. ...

5. ...

6. ...

7. ...

Les assemblages de verbes

Pour exprimer ses goûts

46 Décris les goûts de ces personnages.

	Nick and Emily	Tom	Nina
	♥♥	♥♥♥	✗
	♥	✗	♥♥
	✗	✗✗	♥
	♥	♥♥	✗✗
	♥♥♥	♥	✗
	♥♥♥	♥♥♥	♥♥♥

47 Écris une phrase pour parler de tes goûts. Pense à varier les verbes.

Le choix de l'article

Les articles ø / a / an / the

Besoin d'aide ?
Relis la leçon p. 22 et 68.

48 Complète avec l'article approprié : *a, an, ø, the.*

a. ... Queen Elizabeth was born in 1926.

b. I went to ... United Kingdom last summer.

c. Would you like ... cup of tea?

d. Could I just have ... water please? I would also like ... apple.

e. Do you like ... cats?

49 Complète les phrases suivantes avec *a, an, ø, the.*

a. Our trip in London was fantastic! We saw ... Big Ben, ... Tower of London and ... Tower Bridge.

b. Have you ever been to ... United States of America?

c. Mia is ... English teacher and Simon is ... P.E teacher.

d. Melanie plays ... piano very well.

e. ... *Secret Life of Pets* is ... fun movie!

Le choix de l'adjectif démonstratif

This / That / These

50 Choisis entre *this, that* ou *these.*

[At a party]

– You know what? Jina is here!
– Who's ... ?
– You don't know her? Hang on, I'll introduce you! Jina, ... is Paul. Paul, ... is Jina.
– Nice to meet you, Jina. Is ... your daughter here?
– Erm no, ... is actually my niece! ... are my daughters!

[In a book shop]

– Excuse me, are ... your glasses?
– Oh yes ... is really kind of you!
– No problem. Are you looking for a book in particular?
– Yes, do you have ... recent book by J. K. Rowling?
– No sorry, but what about ... one here?
– Let's see. Oh, ... illustrations are great! Look at ... monsters! How funny! Ok I'll take it!

Le choix du type de nom

Dénombrables / indénombrables

51 Les noms ci-dessous sont-ils dénombrables ou indénombrables ? Place-les dans le bon sac !

dénombrables — indénombrables

computer – chair – sugar – milk – cherry – glass – juice – apple – fish – cat – purse – cheese – fruit – sausage – peanut – salt – foot – mouse – bread – water – time – salad – music – air – plastic

52 Complète les phrases logiquement avec *a few / a little bit / some / a lot of*.

a. We've got ... rice left. There are 3 packets on the shelf.

b. We're not leaving for long. You only need ... pairs of socks, not so many!

c. "Would you like ... milk in your tea?" "Yes please, just ... ."

d. I can't go out tonight. I've got ... homework to do; two long essays!

Pronoms sujet

Besoin d'aide ? Relis la leçon p. 22.

53 Remplace les phrases suivantes par un pronom sujet.

a. Bryan loves sports. ... is a great tennis player!

b. Will and I don't get on. ... are very different.

c. Kathlyn is very important to me. ... is my best friend.

d. Meg and you should go for a walk. ... need a bit of fresh air!

e. The bird is hungry. ... needs to be fed.

f. The teachers are very strict. ... don't tolerate chatting in the classroom.

54 Complète le texte suivant avec un pronom sujet.

Sara and Emily are good friends. ... met at school. Emily is two years older than Sara. ... is 17. ... likes to play baseball with her brother and his best friend Jack. ... is on the school's baseball team!

Sara and I don't know each other very well. ... only met a couple of times. Do ... know her well?

Pronoms complément

Besoin d'aide ? Relis la leçon p. 22.

55 Remplace les mots soulignés par le pronom qui convient.

a. "Do you like cats?"
"Oh yes, I love ... ."

b. "What's the title of your favourite movie?"
"Bad luck! I can't remember ... ."

c. This is my sister. Have you already met ...?

d. John went to the cinema with Mike and I last Saturday. ... liked the film but John didn't. I felt sorry for ... .

56 Complète les phrases avec les pronoms compléments qui conviennent.

a. My parents are so nice! I love ... very dearly!

b. Apparently Sarah was at the party last night. Did you see ... ?

c. My brother won the cup. I'm so happy for... !

d. Don't forget to call your mother! She misses ... so much!

e. I sent Geoffrey a message. He will come with ... to Disneyland!

f. She sent you a postcard. Have you received ... ?

g. Look at this t-shirt! My parents gave it to ... for my birthday.

Pronoms possessifs

Besoin d'aide ? Relis la leçon p. 22.

57 Complète les phrases à l'aide d'un pronom possessif.

a. This book is ... . My mother gave it to me.

b. John, it's not my fault. It's ... . You broke my glasses!

c. "Cecily has forgotten her nice blue shirt."
"Oh yes you're right. It's ... ."

d. "Does this painting belong to your family?"
"Yes, it's ... ."

e. "I think Sam and Charlie have left their coats behind."
"No, don't worry they're not ... ."

f. "Is this your dog's toy?"
"Oh yes it's ... ."

58 Il est temps que les triplés Jamie, Josh et Joy rangent leur chambre. Complète l'échange avec leur père Andy.

Andy: Whose socks are these?

Jamie: There are blue stripes on them. They're Josh's.

Josh: Err... yes, sorry these are ... socks.

Andy: And what about this shirt? Is it ... as well?

Josh: No, it's not ... ! This is a girl's shirt. It's Joy's! And this is ... tee-shirt as well.

Andy: Alright, alright! And these books? Whose books are these?

Jamie: They are ... books, dad. You gave them to us for Christmas.

Josh: And dad! Whose bag is it? Isn't it yours actually?

Andy: Yes, it is ... bag. What is it doing here? Joy, is this ... dress? And what about all these shoes here?

Joy: Obviously the dress is ..., but the shoes belong to the boys. And these are ... slippers as well.

Pronoms relatifs

Besoin d'aide ?
Relis la leçon p. 54.

59 Complète les phrases à l'aide d'un pronom relatif.

a. This is the cat ... bit me! Be careful!

b. The girl ... is sitting over there is my best friend, Emma.

c. The man ... owns the sweetshop is my neighbour.

d. I love the pants ... you bought yesterday.

e. "Could you pass me my scarf please?"
"You mean the one ... is on the chair?"

f. The kids ... are playing football are my nephews.

60 Relie les phrases en utilisant un pronom relatif.

a. John was wearing a cap. It was too big for him.

b. There is a new pupil in our class. He is very friendly.

c. I met a girl. She can speak five languages!

d. We have new neighbours. They have a trampoline in their garden!

e. She saw an exhibition. It was about pirates.

Noms composés

Besoin d'aide ?
Relis la leçon p. 82.

61 Associe ces noms par paires pour former des noms composés. Essaie ensuite d'en inventer un nouveau et de l'illustrer !

cake snow cow butter

fly rise flake hair lip

step boy man cup cut

sun snow stick foot

62 Retrouve autant de noms composés que tu peux dans ce nuage de mots.

birth kick end
thunder table book
week fighter noon storm after
time sitter baby side
fire day case bed

Composés de *some* / *any* / *no*

63 Complète ces phrases avec *some*, *any* ou *no*.

a. You'll have to wait for quite a while. Would you like ...thing to read?

b. My foot hurts! I've got ...thing in my shoe.

c. I'm thirsty. Is there ...thing to drink?

d. My car is not working. I can't go ...where.

e. This place isn't very interesting. There's ...thing to see.

f. ...one rang at the door but I was in my bath.

L'adjectif

Besoin d'aide ?
Relis la leçon p. 22.

Les différents choix possibles

64 **Décris ce monstre. Sois le plus précis possible (couleur, taille, impression produite...).**

65 **Complète cet autoportrait en ajoutant les adjectifs proposés au bon endroit. Puis, à ton tour, décris-toi afin que quelqu'un qui ne t'a jamais vu(e) puisse te reconnaître parmi d'autres personnes.**

My name is Sarah. I am very ... . I have ... hair. It is ... and ... . Today, I'm wearing a ... shirt, a skirt and ... heels. I'm going to the market with my ... , ... shopping bag.

Le génitif

Établir des liens de parenté

Besoin d'aide ?
Relis la leçon p. 90.

66 **Observe cet arbre généalogique et complète les phrases ci-dessous.**

a. Ashley is ... daughter.

b. Derek and Jennifer are ... children.

c. Jennifer is ... sister.

d. Tim is ... father.

e. Derek is Daphne's ... .

f. Phyllis is ... grandmother.

g. Brian is ... son.

Exprimer la possession

67 **Observe les illustrations puis restitue les objets à chacun.**

e.g. *hat* → This is Tom's hat.

a. bike

b. skateboard

c. rollerblades

d. scooter

68 **Fais des phrases pour indiquer à qui appartient chaque objet.**

e. g. • *This is Tom's hat*
• *This hat is Tom's*

Adjectifs possessifs

Besoin d'aide ?
Relis la leçon p. 22.

69 **Complète avec un adjectif possessif.**

a. Bella is so lucky! She has a dog and a cat. ... dog is very cute: it wags ... tail when it sees her.

b. I know you often go to the swimming pool. Do you open ... eyes under water?

c. Hello, ... name is Julien. What about you, what's ... name?

70 **Complète avec l'adjectif possessif approprié.**

a. John is at the swimming pool but he has forgotten ... swimming cap!

b. Mark and Linda are moving to New York. They are packing ... suitcases.

c. Brenda likes pop music. ... favourite band is U2.

d. "Where is ... dog?"
"It's in ... doghouse."

e. Sorry, I can't read, I haven't got ... glasses.

f. Lucinda and I are fond of the USA. .... favourite destination is Chicago, we love The Bean!

Les prépositions

Les prépositions de lieu

Besoin d'aide ?
Relis le vocabulaire p. 80.

71 **Observe l'image. Avec ton voisin, situez à tour de rôle un maximum d'objets!**

Aide lexicale

wardrobe = armoire
bedside table = table de chevet
slippers = chaussons
candlestick = bougeoir

72 **Complète ce texte avec les prépositions suivantes :**
next to – behind – through – in – on top of

To get to my friend Lucy's place, you need to walk ... the forest and climb ... the hill. Lucy lives ... a farm where her family buys fresh milk. ... her house, ... the garden, there are some swings. It's a fun place to be!

Les prépositions de temps

73 **Choisis la bonne préposition pour compléter ces phrases.**
in – at – on

a. I was born ... August: ... August 9th, 2003.

b. They are moving to Los Angeles ... Easter.

c. Tomorrow you start school ... 8.30.

d. They enjoy going out ... night.

74 Choisis la bonne préposition pour compléter ces phrases.

in – at – on

a. Jack will be ... time: he will arrive ... 3 p.m. as usual.

b. I never work ... weekends because I prefer spending time with my family.

c. Amy will go to London ... Christmas day. She will leave ... the morning and she will come back the week after.

d. My sister was born ... July the 1st, 2001.

e. ... the 18th century, people had no phones!

Les adverbes

De fréquence

Besoin d'aide ? Relis la leçon p. 44.

75 Remets les mots dans l'ordre pour obtenir une phrase bien construite !

a. usually / goes / on / Charlie / school / to / foot.

b. watches / at / Izzy / TV / never / home.

c. ? / Arthur / Merlin / King / do / and / agree / always

d. is / Sam / she / up / sometimes / grumpy / when / wakes.

e. Harry / late / Potter / ? / class / is / often / for / potions / his

De manière

Besoin d'aide ? Relis la leçon p. 44.

76 À partir de la liste de mots ci-dessous, complète les phrases suivantes.

loudly – carefully – suddenly – badly – late –straight – fluently

a. Stop laughing so ... please!

b. My mother wants me to go ... home after school.

c. He speaks Spanish ... because his dad is from Madrid.

d. ... , there was a terrible noise.

e. They keep arriving ... at school.

f. Think ... and give the correct answer.

g. His dog barks all day long, he's ... behaved.

Le choix du quantifieur

Les nombres ordinaux et cardinaux

Besoin d'aide ? Relis la leçon p. 36.

77 Écoute et recopie ce que tu as entendu. Track 149

a.	10	25	35
b.	39	13	59
c.	77	67	83
d.	1st	11th	21st
e.	83rd	87	83
f.	15th	50	15
g.	64th	54th	74

78 Complète les mots-croisés suivants.

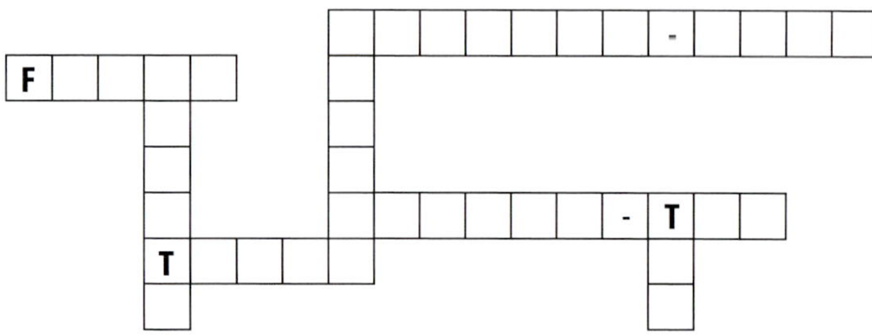

À trouver : 50 – 20 – 75 – 92 – 3rd – 2nd – 10

Quantifier les noms

79 Choisis le bon quantifieur :

any – some – much – many

a. How ... time do you need in order to do the shopping?

b. I'd like ... olive oil with my salad please.

c. ... absent today?

d. How ... money do you have left?

e. There are too ... people waiting, let's come back tomorrow.

f. There isn't ... milk left in the fridge.

g. ... of us won't go to the pool today.

Le comparatif

Besoin d'aide ? Relis la leçon p. 100.

Les adjectifs courts et les adjectifs longs

80 Classe les adjectifs dans la bonne colonne puis indique leur comparatif. Utilise ensuite trois d'entre eux pour comparer des éléments de ton choix.

small – helpful – obedient – strong – patient – great – caring – reliable – cheap – fast

	Adjectifs courts	Adjectifs longs
Adjectif:		
Comparatif:		

Le choix du comparatif

81 Complète le descriptif donné par le vendeur de ce skateboard.

This skateboard is very solid. It will stay in good condition much ... *(long)* than any other skateboard. It is also ... *(resistant)* to snow and ice than the other brands: its wheels are made of a special material that avoids slipping. It is not ... *(heavy)* ... it looks: only 1 kg! That will enable you to go ... *(fast)* and ... *(far)*. If you would like to buy it, I can make it ... *(expensive)* for you.

82 Compare ces animaux.

(young)

(affectionate)

(fat)

(fast)

83 Compare ces éléments.

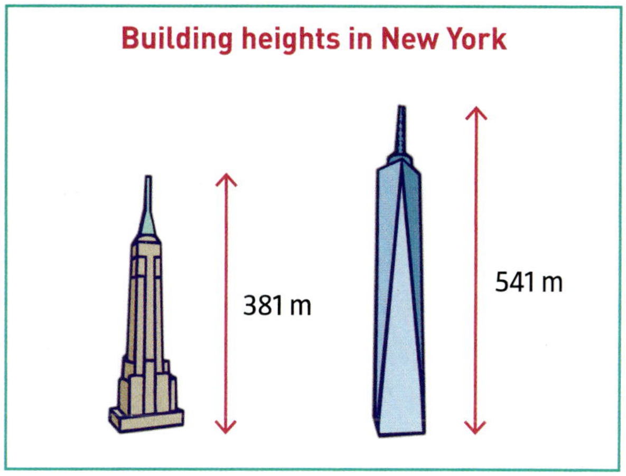

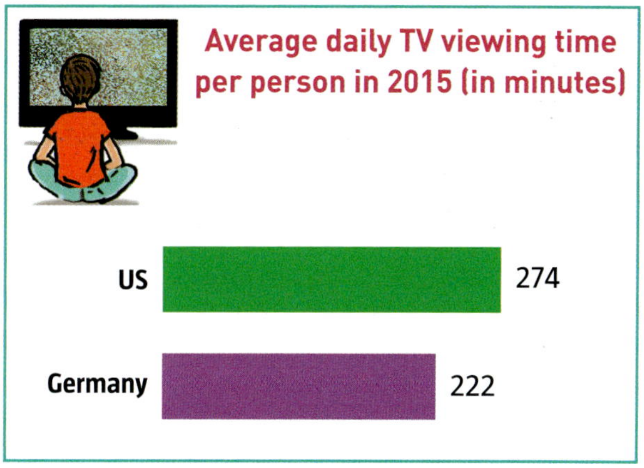

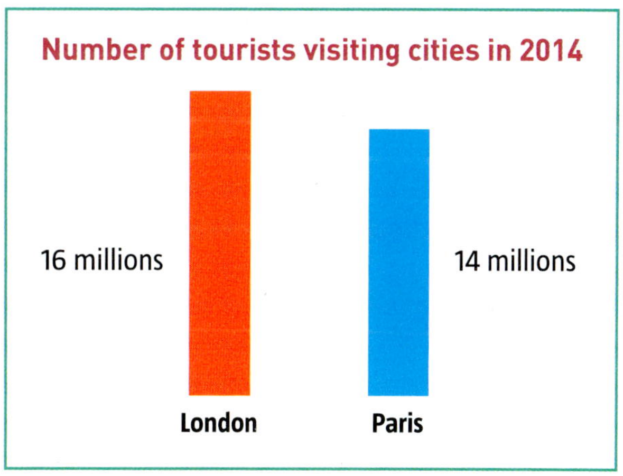

84 Compare les personnages suivants:

a. Harry Potter / Voldemort (nice)

b. Asterix / Obelix (strong)

c. Shrek / Fiona (rude)

d. Lisa Simpson / Bart Simpson (intelligent)

Le superlatif

Besoin d'aide ?
Relis la leçon p. 90.

85 Transforme ces phrases en utilisant le superlatif de supériorité.

e.g. *I visited a great exhibition* → I visited the greatest exhibition.

a. I'm going to see a good movie →

b. I married a wonderful actor →

c. My brother bought a fast car →

d. She gave me a beautiful flower →

e. We live in a high building →

f. I got a bad mark →

86 Complète avec le superlatif de supériorité.

I think New York is ... *(beautiful)* city in the world. You can eat ... *(good)* hot-dogs and see ... *(high)* buildings.

New-yorkers are ... *(lucky)* people in the world, they can watch the ... *(great)* shows whenever they want. They can also have a walk in one of ... *(big)* parks in the world: Central Park!

87 Utilise les adjectifs et noms proposés pour exprimer tes goûts. Utilise le superlatif de supériorité.

e. g. *Interesting / book → The most interesting book is* Charlie and the Chocolate Factory.

a. Funny / film →

b. Interesting / school subject →

c. Good / sport →

d. Useful / invention →

e. Great / day of the week →

L'heure

88 Quelle est l'heure indiquée sur ces cadrans ?

a. 2 : 20
- ☐ Twenty past two
- ☐ Twenty to two
- ☐ Two past twenty

b. 3 : 30
- ☐ Thirteen past three
- ☐ Three to thirty
- ☐ Half past three

c. 4 : 45
- ☐ Quarter past four
- ☐ Quarter to five
- ☐ Forty five past four

d. 8 : 15
- ☐ Quarter to eight
- ☐ Eight past quarter
- ☐ Quarter past eight

e. 9 : 00
- ☐ Nine o'clock
- ☐ Nine past zero
- ☐ Half past nine

89 Dessine les horloges correspondant aux heures suivantes :

a. Half past six

b. Twelve past four

c. Twenty-five to nine

d. Midday

e. Five to five

f. Ten past one

g. Ten o'clock

h. Half past five

90 Quelle heure est-il ?

a

b
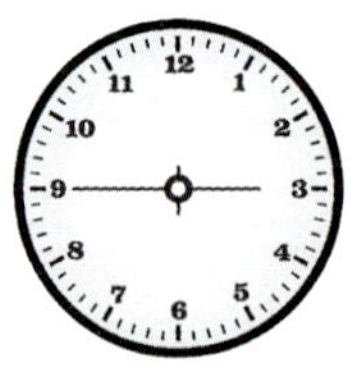

c

d

e
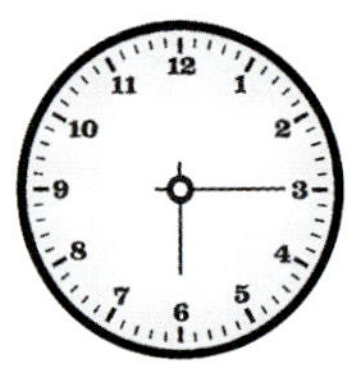

f
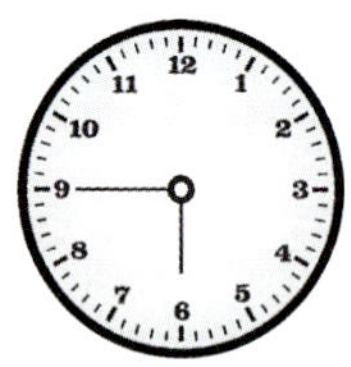

g

Lexique

Ce lexique reprend et enrichit le vocabulaire rencontré dans les chapitres du manuel.

→ Consulte-le pour :

- rechercher un mot au moment de réaliser une activité ou une tâche,
- enrichir ton vocabulaire sur un sujet donné,
- t'adresser à la classe à l'oral.

→ Si tu as besoin de rechercher d'autres mots :

utilise un dictionnaire papier ou un dictionnaire en ligne, par exemple :
www.wordreference.com ou www.thefreedictionary.com.

→ Prends l'habitude d'apprendre les mots avec leur prononciation :

tu peux les écouter sur un dictionnaire de prononciation en ligne, par exemple www.howjsay.com.

Lexique

Basics

Numbers

one	un
two	deux
three /θriː/	trois
four	quatre
five /faɪv/	cinq
six	six
seven	sept
eight /eɪt/	huit
nine	neuf
ten	dix
eleven /ɪ'levn/	onze
twelve	douze
thir**teen**	treize
four**teen**	quatorze
fif**teen**	quinze
six**teen**	seize
seven**teen**	dix-sept
eigh**teen**	dix-huit
nine**teen**	dix-neuf
twenty	vingt
thirty /ɜː/	trente
forty	quarante
fifty	cinquante
sixty	soixante
seventy	soixante-dix
eighty	quatre-vingt
ninety	quatre-vingt-dix
one **hun**dred /'hʌndrəd/	cent
one **thou**sand /'θaʊzənd/	mille

Time

quarter past /'kwɔːtə/	et quart
quarter to	moins le quart
o'clock	(heure pile)
half past /hɑːf/	et demi
before ≠ **af**ter /ɪ/	avant ≠ après
during /'djʊərɪŋ/	pendant
for *(+ durée)*	pendant
in *(+ mois ou année)*	en
in the after**noon**	l'après-midi
in the **eve**ning /'iːvnɪŋ/	le soir
in the **mor**ning	le matin
on *(+ jour ou date)*	le
to**mor**row /tə'mɒrəʊ/	demain
week	semaine
yesterday	hier

Calendar

Days of the week

Monday	lundi
Tuesday /'tjuːzdeɪ/	mardi
Wednesday /'wenzdeɪ/	mercredi
Thursday /'θɜːzdeɪ/	jeudi
Friday /'fraɪdeɪ/	vendredi
Saturday	samedi
Sunday	dimanche

Months

January	janvier
February	février
March /mɑːtʃ/	mars

April /ˈeɪprəl/	avril
May	mai
June	juin
July /dʒuˈlaɪ/	juillet
August /ˈɔːgʌst/	août
Sep**tem**ber	septembre
Oc**to**ber	octobre
No**vem**ber	novembre
De**cem**ber /ɪ/	décembre

Seasons

autumn (UK) / fall (US) /ˈɔːtəm/	automne
spring	printemps
summer	été
winter	hiver

Colours

beige	beige
black	noir
brown /aʊ/	marron
dark blue	bleu foncé
dark green	vert foncé
grey /eɪ/	gris
lavender	lavande, mauve
light blue /laɪt/	bleu clair
light green	vert clair
ma**roon** /məˈruːn/	bordeaux
orange	orange
pink	rose
purple, **vi**olet /pɜːpl/ /ˈvaɪələt/	violet
red	rouge
turquoise /ˈtɜːkwɔɪz/	turquoise
white /aɪ/	blanc
yellow	jaune

School

School supplies

backpack	sac à dos
binder /aɪ/	classeur
board /bɔːrd/	tableau
book	livre
coloured **pen**cil	crayon de couleur
compass	compas
com**pu**ter	ordinateur
copybook = **note**book	cahier
cor**rec**tion fluid	blanc correcteur
day **plan**ner/**dia**ry	agenda
desk	bureau
felt pen	stylo feutre
folder /ˈfəʊldə/	classeur
fountain pen /ˈfaʊntɪnˈpen/	stylo plume
glue stick	colle
highlighter /ˈhaɪlaɪtə/	surligneur
hole punch	perforactrice
laptop	ordinateur portable
marker	marqueur
(piece of) **pa**per	(feuille de) papier
pencil /ˈpensl/	crayon
pencil case	trousse
pencil **shar**pener	taille crayons
rubber /ˈrʌbər/	gomme
ruler	règle
schoolbag	cartable
scissors	ciseaux
tape	scotch

textbook	manuel scolaire
workbook	cahier d'exercices

People at school

classmate / **part**ner /eɪ/	camarade de classe
schoolmate	camarade d'école
head / **head**master / **prin**cipal	principal
pupil / **stu**dent /ˈpjuːpl/	élève
staff	personnel (n)
teacher	professeur

Places

classroom	salle de classe
playground	cour de récréation
school canteen / cafe**te**ria /kæfɪˈtɪərɪə/	cantine
school	école
sports ground	terrain de sport
sports hall / gym**na**sium /dʒɪmˈneɪzɪəm/	gymnase

People and characters

Family

aunt /ɑːnt/	tante
brother	frère
child / **chil**dren /tʃaɪld/ /ˈtʃɪldrən/	enfant /enfants
cousin /ˈkʌzn/	cousin
daughter /ˈdɔːtə/	fille
father /ˈfɑːðə/	père
grandfather, grandpa	grand-père, papi
grandmother, grandma	grand-mère, mamie
grandparents	grands-parents
half-brother / **half**-sister /ˈhɑːf/	demi-frère / demi-sœur
husband /ˈhʌzbənd/	mari
mother /ˈmʌðə/	mère
parents /ˈpɛərənts/	parents
son /sʌn/	fils
stepfather	beau-père
stepmother	belle-mère
uncle /ˈʌŋkl/	oncle
wife /waɪf/	femme

Pirates

anchor /ˈæŋkə/	ancre
at**tack**	attaquer
beard /bɪəd/	barbe
be**low** deck	pont inférieur
bury /ˈberɪ/	enterrer
cannon	canon
captain	capitaine
capture /ˈkæptʃə/	capturer
crew /kruː/	équipage
cutlass	coutelas

deck	pont
dig	creuser
dis**co**ver	découvrir
explore	explorer
fishing rod	canne à pêche
flag	drapeau
go on a trip	faire un voyage
gold	or
island /ˈaɪlənd/	île
look for	chercher
matey /ˈmeɪtɪ/	mon pote
menacing	menaçant
ocean /ˈəʊʃn/	océan
parrot	perroquet
plank /plæŋk/	planche
rob	voler
ruthless /ˈruːθlɪs/	impitoyable
sail /seɪl/	voguer / naviguer
sailor	matelot / marin
scary /ˈskɛərɪ/	effrayant
sea	mer
search	chercher
shipwreck /ˈʃɪprek/	épave
skull	crâne
spade	pelle
spyglass	longue-vue
steal	voler
sword /sɔːd/	épée
telescope	téléscope
travel	voyager
treasure /ˈtreʒə/	trésor
treasure chest /ˈtʃest/	coffre au trésor
treasure map	carte au trésor

Describing

People

Body parts

arms	bras
belly	ventre
body / **tor**so	corps / torse
ears	oreilles
eyes	yeux
face	visage
feet	pieds
hands	mains
head	tête
legs	jambes
mouth	bouche
nails	ongles
nose	nez
skin	peau
tooth / teeth	dent / dents

Personality

arrogant	arrogant
awesome / great / a**ma**zing /ˈɔːsəm/	genial, super, extraordinaire
bully	brute
caring	attentionné
clever	intelligent
ef**fi**cient /ɪˈfɪʃənt/	efficace
hard-**wor**king	travailleur
helpful	serviable, utile
honest /ˈɒnɪst/	honnête
lazy	fainéant
mean /miːn/	méchant
nice / kind	gentil
o**be**dient	obéissant
out**go**ing	sociable
patient /ˈpeɪʃnt/	patient

polite	poli
responsible /rɪ'spɒnsɪbl/	responsable
rude /ruːd/	grossier
selfish	égoïste
shy	timide
smart	intelligent
stubborn /'stʌbən/	têtu
talkative /'tɔːkətɪv/	bavard
touchy /'tʌtʃɪ/	sensible
trickster	farceur

Feelings

angry	en colère,furieux
bored /bɔːd/	qui s'ennuie
cautious /'kɔːʃəs/	prudent
confident	assuré /confiant / sûr de soi
cross	fâché, en colère
curious /'kjʊərɪs/	curieux
disappointed /dɪsə'pɔɪntɪd/	déçu
disgusted /dɪs'gʌstɪd/	dégoûté
happy	heureux / content
hungry	affamé
jealous /'dʒeləs/	jaloux
joyful	joyeux
lonely /'ləʊnlɪ/	seul
mad	furieux
miserable /'mɪzərəbl/	malheureux
nervous /'nɜːvəs/	nerveux
optimistic	optimiste
pessimistic	pessimiste
sad	triste
scared	effrayé
thirsty /'θɜːstɪ/	assoiffé
tired /'taɪəd/	fatigué

Tastes

delicious /dɪ'lɪʃəs/	délicieux
disgusting /dɪs'gʌstɪŋ/	dégoûtant
mouth-watering /'maʊθ/	appétissant
tasty	savoureux

Relashionships

acquaintance /ə'kweɪntəns/	connaissance
buddy / mate	pote
friend	ami
friendship	amitié
pal	copain / copine

Activities and habits

Daily routine

Getting ready for school

be late ≠ be on time	être en retard ≠ être à l'heure
do your homework	faire ses devoirs
get dressed	s'habiller
get ready	s'aprêter
get up	se lever
go to school	aller à l'école
grow up	grandir
have breakfast /'brekfəst/	prendre son petit-déjeuner
lay down	s'allonger
look for	chercher
pack your schoolbag	faire son cartable

pre**pa**re /prɪˈpeə/	preparer
roll out of bed /rəʊl/ /aʊt/	tomber de son lit
snore /snɔː/	ronfler
take a **show**er /eɪ/ /ˈʃaʊə/	prendre une douche
wake up	se réveiller

Sports

(ice) **ho**ckey /ˈhɒkɪ/	hockey (sur glace)
ath**le**tics /æθˈletɪks/	athlétisme
baseball	base-ball
basketball	basket-ball
boxing	boxe
cricket /ɪ/	cricket
cycling /ˈsaɪklɪŋ/	cyclisme
football / soccer /ˈsɑkə/	football
rugby	rugby
swimming	natation
tennis	tennis
volleyball /ˈvɒlɪbɔːl/	volley-ball

Having fun

browse the **in**ternet /braʊz/	naviguer sur internet
chat with a friend	bavarder avec un ami
listen to **mu**sic	écouter de la musique
play an **in**strument	jouer d'un instrument
play **vi**deo **games**	jouer à des jeux vidéos
read	lire
send text messages	envoyer des sms
watch TV / a DVD	regarder la télévision / regarder un DVD

Jobs

baker	boulanger
builder /ˈbɪldə/	maçon
butcher /ˈbʊtʃə/	boucher
dentist	dentiste
doctor	docteur
fireman / **fire**fighter /ˈfaɪəfaɪtə/	pompier
hairdresser	coiffeur
hunter /ˈhʌntə/	chasseur
lawyer /ˈlɔːjə/	avocat
nurse /nɜːs/	infirmier
op**ti**cian /ɒpˈtɪʃən/	optician
pho**to**grapher	photographe
po**lice**man	policier
postman	facteur
secretary /ˈsekrətrɪ/	secrétaire
singer /ˈsɪŋə/	chanteur
storyteller	conteur (écrivain)
teacher	professeur
vet	vétérinaire
waiter /eɪ/	serveur

Technology

Building a robot

arti**fi**cial in**tel**ligence	l'intelligence artificielle
chip	puce
language	langage
memory	mémoire
wheel	roue
write a **pro**gram	écrire un programme

Material

glass	verre / en verre
leather /ˈleðə/	cuir / en cuir
metal /ˈmetl/	métal / en métal
paper	papier / en papier
plastic	plastique / en plastique
wood / **wood**en /ˈwʊdn/	bois / en bois
wool / **wool**en /ˈwʊlən/	laine / en laine

Clothes and accessories

belt	ceinture
blouse /blaʊz/	chemisier
boots /uː/	bottes
bracelet /ˈbreɪslɪt/	bracelet
cardigan	gilet
coat /kəʊt/	manteau
dress	robe
earrings /ˈɪərɪŋz/	boucles d'oreille
flip-flops	tongs
glasses	lunettes
gloves	gants
hoodie /ˈhʊdɪ/	sweat à capuche
jacket /ˈdʒækɪt/	veste
jeans	jean
jumper /ˈdʒʌmpə/	pull
necklace /ˈneklɪs/	collier
polo shirt /ˈpəʊləʊ/	polo
ring	bague
scarf	écharpe
shirt	chemise
shoes	chaussures
shorts	short
skirt	jupe
socks	chaussettes
swim cap	bonnet de bain
swimsuit /ˈswɪmsuːt/	maillot de bain
tank top	débardeur
tie /taɪ/	cravate
tights /taɪts/	collants
towel /ˈtaʊəl/	serviette
tracksuit /suːt/	survêtement
trainers	baskets
trousers	pantalon
T-shirt	tee-shirt
underwear /ˈʌndəweə/	sous-vêtements
uniform /ˈjuːnɪfɔːm/	uniforme

House

attic	grenier
basement	cave
bathroom /ˈbæθruːm/	salle de bain
bathtub /tʌb/	baignoire
bed	lit
bedroom	chambre
blanket	couverture
bookcase	bibliothèque (meuble)
carpet /ˈkɑːpɪt/	tapis
ceiling /ˈsiːlɪŋ/	plafond
chair /tʃeə/	chaise

closet	placard
couch /kaʊtʃ/	canapé
curtain /ˈkɜːtn/	rideau
desk	bureau (meuble)
dining room	salle à manger
door /dɔː/	porte
fan	éventail
floor / **sto**rey	étage
front door / back door	porte de devant / de derrière
furniture /ˈfɜːnɪtʃə/	meuble
garage /ˈgærɑːʒ/	garage
garden	jardin
gate /eɪ/	portail
hall /hɔːl/	entrée (vestibule)
hallway	couloir
house /haʊs/	maison
key /kiː/	clé
kitchen	cuisine
lamp	lampe
living room	salon
lock	verrou
mirror /ˈmɪrə/	miroir
office	bureau
picture	photo
porch /pɔːtʃ/	veranda / porche
roof	toit
room	pièce
shelf	étagère
sink	évier / lavabo
sofa	canapé
staircase	cage d'escaliers
stairs /steəz/	escaliers
table	table
tile	tuile / carreau
toilet /ˈtɔɪlɪt/	toilette
wall /wɔːl/	mur
window	fenêtre

Travelling abroad

Countries

Algeria /ælˈdʒɪərɪə/	l'Algérie
Au**stra**lia /eɪ/	l'Australie
Canada /ˈkænədə/	le Canada
China /ˈtʃaɪnə/	la Chine
Eire /ˈeərə/	la République d'Irlande
England /ˈɪŋglənd/	l'Angleterre
France	la France
Germany	l'Allemagne
Great **Bri**tain /ˈbrɪtən/	la Grande-Bretagne
India	l'Inde
Ireland /ˈaɪələnd/	l'Irlande
Italy	l'Italie
Ja**mai**ca	la Jamaïque
Ja**pan** /dʒəˈpæn/	le Japon
Mo**ro**cco /məˈrɒkəʊ/	le Maroc
New **Zea**land	la Nouvelle-Zélande
Northern Ireland /ˈnɔːðən/ /ˈaɪələnd/	l'Irlande du Nord
Scotland	l'Écosse

South Africa	l'Afrique du Sud
Spain	l'Espagne
The Netherlands	les Pays-Bas
The United Kingdom /juː'naɪtɪd/	le Royaume-Uni
The United States of America (USA)	les États-Unis d'Amérique
Ulster /'ʌlstə/	l'Irlande du Nord

Nationalities

Algerian /æl'dʒɪərɪən/	algérien
American /ə'merɪkən/	américain
Australian /eɪ/	australien
British	britannique
British Irish /'aɪrɪʃ/	irlandais (pour l'Irlande du Nord uniquement)
Canadian /kə'neɪdɪən/	canadien
Chinese /tʃaɪ'niːz/	chinois
Dutch	néerlandais
English	anglais
French	français
German	allemand
Indian	indien
Irish /'aɪrɪʃ/	irlandais
Italian	italien
Jamaican	jamaicain
Japanese /dʒæpə'niːz/	japonais
Moroccan /mə'rɒkən/	marocain
New Zealander	neo-zélandais
Scottish	écossais
South African	sud-africain
Spanish	espagnol

In a city

airport /'ɛərpɔːt/	aéroport
avenue / street /'ævənuː/	avenue / rue
bakery /'beɪkərɪ/	boulangerie
bank	banque
block	pâté de maison
bookshop / bookstore	librairie
borough /'bʌrə/	un quartier
bridge	pont
building /'bɪldɪŋ/	bâtiment
car park	parking
chemist's (UK) / drugstore (US)	pharmacie
cinema	cinéma
crossroad /'krɒːsrəʊd/	carrefour
crowd /kraʊd/	foule
dazzled /'dæzəld/	ébloui
downtown /daʊn'taʊn/	centre-ville
hospital	hôpital
hotel	hotel
house	maison
ice rink	une patinoire
library /'laɪbrərɪ/	bibliothèque
look around	regarder autour
loud /laʊd/	bruyant
market	marché
monument /'mɒːnjʊmənt/	un monument
musical /'mjuːzɪkl/	comédie musicale
noise	bruit
park	parc
police station	commissariat de police

post office	bureau de poste
restaurant /'restərɒ:nt/	restaurant
river	rivière
shop / store	magasin
show	spectacle
sidewalk /'saɪdwɔ:k/	trottoir
skyscraper /'skaɪskreɪpə/	gratte-ciel
spot	endroit
stadium /'steɪdɪəm/	stade
stage	scène
station	gare / station
church / ca**the**dral /kə'θi:drəl/	église / cathédrale
statue /'stætju:/	statue
suburb /'sʌbɜ:b/	banlieue
swimming pool	piscine
theater /'θɪətə/	théâtre / salle de spectacle
tourist office	office du tourisme
town **hall**/ city hall /taʊn'hɔ:l/	hôtel de ville / mairie
town	petite ville
village /'vɪlɪdʒ/	village
visit	visiter
zoo /zu:/	zoo

Money

af**ford** /ə'fɔ:d/	s'offrir, se payer / se permettre d'acheter
be worth /wɜ:θ/	valoir
borrow /'bɒrəʊ/	emprunter
buy /baɪ/	acheter
cash	espèces / argent liquide
cash ma**chine**	distributeur automatique de billets
cheque /tʃek/	addition / chèque
coin /kɔɪn/	pièce de monnaie
cost	coûter
credit card /kɑ:d/	carte de crédit / carte bleue
lend	prêter
note (UK) / bill (US)	billet
cent	centime
piggy bank	tirelire
poor /pʊə/	pauvre
the pound / one pound	la Livre sterling / une livre
price	prix
purse / **wal**let /pɜ:s/ /'wɒlɪt/	porte-monnaie / portefeuille
rich	riche
safe	coffre-fort
spend	dépenser
waste	gapiller / gâcher
with**draw** cash /wɪð'rɔ:/	retirer de l'argent

Famous places (New York)

aquarium the New York a**qua**rium	aquarium
at**trac**tion: the **Sta**tue of **Li**berty	attraction
bridge: **Broo**klyn Bridge	pont
castle: /'kɑːsl/ **Bel**vedere **Cas**tle /'belvɪdɪə/	château
mu**seum**: Metro**po**litan Museum of Art	musée

Directions

East /iːst/	est
North /nɔːθ/	nord
South /saʊθ/	sud
West /west/	ouest

Location

a**bove**	au-dessus de
be**hind** /bɪˈhaɪnd/	derrière
be**tween**	entre
down	en bas / vers le bas
in	dans
in the middle (of)	au centre (de)
next to	à côté de
on / on top of	par-dessus
through /θruː/	à travers
up	en haut / vers le haut

Means of transport

bicycle / bike	vélo
boat /bəʊt/	bateau
bus / **shut**tle bus /ˈʃʌtlbʌs/	bus / navette
cab	taxi
car	voiture
ferry	ferry
helicopter	hélicoptère
line	ligne (de métro)
lorry / truck	camion
map	carte
motorbike / bike	moto
plane	avion
scooter	scooter / trotinette
subway / **un**derground	métro
subway **sta**tion	station de metro
ticket	ticket
train	train

Organizing and moving

be in a rush /rʌʃ/	être pressé
cross	traverser
get a ride	se faire conduire
go / head for	aller / se rendre
hail a cab /heɪl/	héler
move	déménager
pack **some**one's bags	faire ses valises
start from	partir de
take off	décoller
tour	voyage organisé
travel to	voyager vers
work out / plan a trip	planifier un voyage

Nature

Animals

Pets

bird /bɜːd/	oiseau
cat / **kit**ten	chat / chaton
dog / **pup**py /ʌ/	chien / chiot
fish / fish	poisson / des poissons
goldfish	poisson rouge
guinea pig /ˈgɪnɪpɪg/	cochon d'inde
hamster /ə/	hamster
mouse / mice /maʊs/ /maɪs/	une souris / des souris
parakeet (US) / **bud**gie (GB)	perruche

parrot	perroquet
rabbit	lapin
rat	rat
snake /eɪ/	serpent
turtle / **tor**toise /ˈtɔːtəs/	tortue marine / tortue

Wild animals

alligator	alligator
bear /beə/	ours
bird	oiseau
butterfly	papillon
crocodile	crocodile
deer	cerf
elephant /ˈelɪfənt/	éléphant
gi**raffe** /dʒɪˈrɑːf/	girafe
hippo**po**tamus / hippo	hippopotame
kanga**roo** /kæŋɡəˈruː/	kangourou
lion	lion
monkey /ˈmʌŋki/	singe
panda	panda
possum /ˈpɒsəm/	opossum
rhi**no**ceros / rhino /raɪˈnɒsərəs/	rhinocéros
shark	requin
snake	serpent
tiger	tigre
wolf /wʊlf/	loup
zebra /ˈziːbrə/	zèbre

Animal body parts

claw /klɔː/	griffe
mane	crinière
paw /pɔː/	patte
tail /teɪl/	queue
whiskers	moustaches
wings	ailes

Places

bank	rive
edge /edʒ/	bord (d'un lac) / orée d'un bois
field /fiːld/	champs
grass	herbe
lake /leɪk/	lac
mud /mʌd/	boue
pond	étang / mare
water	eau
woods /wʊdz/	bois

Celebrating

Halloween

appa**ri**tion /æpəˈrɪʃən/	apparition / fantôme
bag	sac
bat	chauve-souris
blood /blʌd/	sang
bones /ˈbəʊnz/	os
broom /bruːm/	balai
candle /ˈkændl/	bougie
candy	bonbons
cape	cape
cauldron /ˈkɔːldrən/	chaudron

cele**bration** /selɪ'breɪʃn/	fête
cemetery / graveyard /'semɪtrɪ/	cimetière
cloak /kləʊk/	cape
coffin	cercueil
costume	costume
creepy	qui donne la chair de poule
death (n.) / **dead** (adj.)	la mort / mort
devil /'devəl/	diable
dreadful / **ho**rrible	effrayant / horrible
dress up	se déguiser
frightening / **sca**ry /'fraɪtnɪŋ/	effrayant
ghost /gəʊst/	fantôme
grave	tombe
haunted house	maison hantée
horror /'hɒrə/	horreur
invi**ta**tion / in**vite**	invitation / inviter
Jack-o'-**lan**tern	citrouille d'halloween
join a **par**ty /dʒɔɪn/	rejoindre une fête
joke /əʊ/	blague
lo**ca**tion / place /ləʊ'keɪʃən/ /eɪ/	lieu
magic	magique
monster	monstre
mummy	mommie
nightmare /'naɪtmeə/	cauchemar
pumpkin	citrouille / potiron
RSVP = re**ply** to an invi**ta**tion	répondre à une invitation
shadow	ombre
shock	choc
skeleton	squelette
spell	sort
spider web	toile d'araignée
spirit	esprit
throw / launch a **par**ty	donner une fête
trick-or-**treat**	un bonbon ou un sort
wand	baguette magique
wicked /'wɪkɪd/	méchant / super
witch	sorcière
zombie /'zɒmbɪ/	zombie

The past

anni**ver**sary /ænɪ'vɜːsərɪ/	anniversaire (de mariage)
celebrate	célébrer
co**mme**morate	commémorer
commemo**ra**tion	commémoration
date	date
des**cribe**	décrire
e**vent**	événement
famous	célèbre, connu
great /eɪ/	grand /super
history	histoire
monarchy /'mɒnəkɪ/	monarchie
story	histoire
timeline	frise chronologique

Memorable people

a**ma**zing	extraordinaire
be born	être né
burry /'berɪ/	enterrer
in**vent**	inventer
known for /nəʊn/	connu pour
live ≠ die /lɪv/	vivre ≠ mourir
memorable /'memərəbl/	memorable

The Great Fire of London

burn /bɜːn/	brûler
destroy / **ravage** /ˈrævɪdʒ/	détruire ravager
es**cape** / flee	s'évader
ex**tin**guish /ɪkˈstɪŋgwɪʃ/	éteindre (le feu)
fire /faɪə/	feu
rescue /ˈreskjuː/	secourir
smoke /əʊ/	fumée
spread	s'étendre / se propager
start / **break** out	commencer / éclater
take place	se passer
threatening /ˈθretnɪŋ/	menaçant

People

ancestors	ancêtres
com**mu**nity /kəˈmjuːnɪtɪ/	communauté
origins	origines
tribe	tribu

In a text

Adverbs

always	toujours
never	jamais
oc**ca**sionally	parfois, quelquefois
often	souvent
quickly	rapidement
rarely /ˈrɛəlɪ/	rarement
slowly /ˈsləʊlɪ/	lentement
sometimes	quelquefois
usually /ˈjuːʒʊəlɪ/	généralement

Link words

al**though** /ɔːlðəʊ/	bien que
and	et
be**cause** /bɪˈkɒz/	parce que
but	mais
contrary to	contrairement à
even though	bien que
in **or**der to	pour / afin que
or	ou
so	donc
when	quand

Words in action

1

Agreeing

- **De**finitly! Abso**lu**tely!
- That's true. That's right. That's con**vin**cing.
- I **agree** with you. I totally **agree**.
- I share your point of view.
- I think so too.
- I see what you mean.
- You're quite right / absolutely right.

Disagreeing

- Not neces**sa**rily! Not at all!
- That's not **al**ways true.
- I don't think so.
- I'm not sure a**bout** that...
- I disa**gree** / I com**ple**tely disa**gree**...
- You could say that, how**e**ver...
- That's one way of **look**ing at it, yet...

2 Giving your opinion

- I think / **believe** / feel / consider / find that...
- To my mind... In my **opinion**... From my point of view... To me...
- As far as I'm con**cerned**...
- What I mean is...
- I am sure that...
- It seems to me that...
- No **mat**ter what you say, I still think that...

3 Talking about a poem

I think my dad is Dracula

I think my dad is Dracula.
I know that sounds insane,
but listen for a moment and
allow me to explain.

We don't live in a castle,
and we never sleep in caves.
But, still, there's something weird
about the way my dad behaves.

I never see him go out
in the daytime when it's light.
He sleeps all day till evening,
then he leaves the house at night.

He comes home in the morning
saying, "Man, I'm really dead!"
He kisses us goodnight, and then
by sunrise he's in bed.

My mom heard my suspicion
and she said, "You're not too swift.
Your father's not a vampire.
He just works the graveyard shift."

A poem by
Kenn Nesbitt, 2009

Title

verse

stanza
→ quatrain (4 lines)

rhyme

poet / author

4 Talking about a picture

1 Presentation of the document (title / artist / material / location)

Kinds of pictures

picture / image / painting / watercolour / photograph / portrait / poster / cartoon / drawing

cover / front page / comic strip

This [image / picture / painting / artwork / sculpture] was [painted / drawn / made]

by [artist] in [date]

It is a picture of...
It is entitled...
The scene takes place in...
The setting is...

2 Description (structure / subject matter) = What?

I can see...
There is / there are...
It shows...
It depicts...
It represents...
We can notice that...

3 Colours

The artist uses warm colours (yellow-red-orange) / cold colours (blue-purple-green).

Its colours are bright / cheerful / dull / rough / lovely / pale / dark.

4 Interpretation (theme / symbols / atmosphere / opinion)

We can suppose...
It seems that...
The atmosphere is...
The picture symbolises...
The artist wants to criticise / express / show...
I think / believe / am sure that...

5 Talking about a website

web page

name of the website

Elon University School of Communications

left panel

Home

Predictions Surveys

KidZone

About the Site

Kids' Predictions for Our Future

title of the article

We asked fifth-graders at Elon Elementary School in North Carolina to write what they think the future will bring. Read some of their ideas, and then write about what you think will happen! Share your ideas with your classmates, friends and family. You never know; they might come true sooner than you think.

introduction

Amanda F. – In the future there will be hoverboards, flying cars and pocket-size computers.

Sydney Y. – We will have robots that clean up after us. The X-box game will be so small it will fit in your watch. Time machines will be amazing.

Jordan W. – There will be enough technology so we can communicate with aliens. There will be a time machine to travel through time. There will be the power to die and come back alive.

Danielle M. – There will be a remote[1] where you type in where you want to go then push the button and you will be there. Also we will have chewing gum that never loses its taste.

Patrick D. – There will be robots that clean your house, walk the dog, make your bed and stuff like that. There will be computers so small you can't see them.

Hannah P. – We will have mini-computers in our clothes – like on the inside of your sleeves. You will also be able to type into your hairbrush how you want your hair to be styled. Robots can get everything for you because you can tell them to make you something.

posts / readers' comments

www. elon.edu

URL (Uniform Resource Locator) / website address

Les verbes irréguliers

Sing sang sung with Fluency MC

Track 150

Voici les verbes irréguliers les plus utilisés. Apprends-les avec leur prononciation.

Infinitif		Prétérit		Participe Passé		Traduction
be	/biː/	was/were	/wɒz/ /wɜː/	been	/biːn/	être
beat	/biːt/	beat	/biːt/	beaten	/biːtn/	battre
become	/bɪˈkʌm/	became	/bɪˈkeɪm/	become	/bɪˈkʌm/	devenir
begin	/bɪˈɡɪn/	began	/bɪˈɡæn/	begun	/bɪˈɡʌn/	commencer
bite	/baɪt/	bit	/bɪt/	bitten	/bɪtn/	mordre
blow	/bləʊ/	blew	/bluː/	blown	/bləʊn/	souffler
break	/breɪk/	broke	/brəʊk/	broken	/ˈbrəʊkn/	casser
bring	/brɪŋ/	brought	/brɔːt/	brought	/brɔːt/	apporter
build	/bɪld/	built	/bɪlt/	built	/bɪlt/	construire
burn	/bɜːn/	burnt	/bɜːnt/	burnt	/bɜːnt/	brûler
buy	/baɪ/	bought	/bɔːt/	bought	/bɔːt/	acheter
catch	/kætʃ/	caught	/kɔːt/	caught	/kɔːt/	attraper
choose	/tʃuːz/	chose	/tʃəʊz/	chosen	/ˈtʃəʊzn/	choisir
come	/kʌm/	came	/keɪm/	come	/kʌm/	venir
cost	/kɒst/	cost	/kɒst/	cost	/kɒst/	coûter
cut	/kʌt/	cut	/kʌt/	cut	/kʌt/	couper
do	/duː/	did	/dɪd/	done	/dʌn/	faire
dream	/driːm/	dreamt	/dremt/	dreamt	/dremt/	rêver
drink	/drɪŋk/	drank	/dræŋk/	drunk	/drʌŋk/	boire
drive	/draɪv/	drove	/drəʊv/	driven	/drɪvn/	conduire
eat	/iːt/	ate	/eɪt/	eaten	/iːtn/	manger
fall	/fɔːl/	fell	/fel/	fallen	/ˈfɔːlən/	tomber
feel	/fiːl/	felt	/felt/	felt	/felt/	se sentir, toucher
fight	/faɪt/	fought	/fɔːt/	fought	/fɔːt/	se battre
find	/faɪnd/	found	/faʊnd/	found	/faʊnd/	trouver
fly	/flaɪ/	flew	/fluː/	flown	/fləʊn/	voler (oiseau, avion...)
forget	/fəˈget/	forgot	/fəˈgɒt/	forgotten	/fəˈgɒtən/	oublier
get	/get/	got	/gɒt/	got	/gɒt/	obtenir

Infinitif		Prétérit		Participe Passé		Traduction
give	/gɪv/	gave	/geɪv/	given	/'gɪvən/	donner
go	/gəʊ/	went	/went/	gone	/gɒn/	aller
have	/hæv/	had	/hæd/	had	/hæd/	avoir
hear	/hɪə/	heard	/hɜːd/	heard	/hɜːd/	entendre
hide	/haɪd/	hid	/hɪd/	hidden	/'hɪdən/	cacher
hit	/hɪt/	hit	/hɪt/	hit	/hɪt/	frapper
hurt	/hɜːt/	hurt	/hɜːt/	hurt	/hɜːt/	blesser
keep	/kiːp/	kept	/kept/	kept	/kept/	garder
leave	/liːv/	left	/left/	left	/left/	quitter, partir
make	/meɪk/	made	/meɪd/	made	/meɪd/	faire, fabriquer
meet	/miːt/	met	/met/	met	/met/	rencontrer
pay	/peɪ/	paid	/peɪd/	paid	/peɪd/	payer
put	/pʊt/	put	/pʊt/	put	/pʊt/	mettre
read	/riːd/	read	/red/	read	/red/	lire
run	/rʌn/	ran	/ræn/	run	/rʌn/	courir
say	/seɪ/	said	/sed/	said	/sed/	dire
see	/siː/	saw	/sɔː/	seen	/siːn/	voir
send	/send/	sent	/sent/	sent	/sent/	envoyer
shoot	/ʃuːt/	shot	/ʃɒt/	shot	/ʃɒt/	tirer (arme)
shut	/ʃʌt/	shut	/ʃʌt/	shut	/ʃʌt/	fermer
sing	/sɪŋ/	sang	/sæŋ/	sung	/sʌŋ/	chanter
sit	/sɪt/	sat	/sæt/	sat	/sæt/	être assis
sleep	/sliːp/	slept	/slept/	slept	/slept/	dormir
smell	/smel/	smelt	/smelt/	smelt	/smelt/	sentir
speak	/spiːk/	spoke	/spəʊk/	spoken	/'spəʊkən/	parler
take	/teɪk/	took	/tʊk/	taken	/teɪkən/	prendre
tell	/tel/	told	/təʊld/	told	/təʊld/	dire, raconter
think	/θɪŋk/	thought	/θɔːt/	thought	/θɔːt/	penser
understand	/ʌndə'stænd/	understood	/ʌndə'stʊd/	understood	/ʌndə'stʊd/	comprendre
wake	/weɪk/	woke	/wəʊk/	woken	/'wəʊkən/	réveiller
win	/wɪn/	won	/wʌn/	won	/wʌn/	gagner
write	/raɪt/	wrote	/rəʊt/	written	/'rɪtən/	écrire

Références iconographiques :

(h) : Alexander Raths/Fotolia ; **(bm) :** Bloomberg/Getty Images/Softbank Robotics ; **(bd) :** Jon Arnold Images/ hemis.fr ; **(bg) :** Westend61 GmbH / Alamy Stock Photo ; **11, 4(h)** Yuri_Arcurs/Istock ; **12 (1) :** Little Miss Tiny/Copyright © 2017 THOIP (a Sanrio compagny) ; **12 (2) :** Mr.Skinny/Copyright © 2017 THOIP (a Sanrio compagny) ; **12 (3) :** Mr.Grumpy/ Copyright © 2017 THOIP (a Sanrio compagny) ; **12 (4) :** Little Miss Fabulous/Copyright © 2017 THOIP (a Sanrio compagny) ; **12 (5) :** Mr.Funny/Copyright © 2017 THOIP (a Sanrio compagny) ; **12 (6) :** Mr.Lazy/Copyright © 2017 THOIP (a Sanrio compagny) ; **12 (7) :** Mr.Tall/Copyright © 2017 THOIP (a Sanrio compagny) ; **12 (8) :** Little Miss Shy/Copyright © 2017 THOIP (a Sanrio compagny) ; **12 (9) :** Mr.Clever/Copyright © 2017 THOIP (a Sanrio compagny) ; **13** Par les élèves de Helen Javot Chadoeuf ; **13, 16, 28, 36, 61** Geoatlas/ Graphi.org ; **13 (hd) :** John Shearer/Getty Images ; **14 (bd), 19 (hd)** Alvin Ho by Leonore Looks/LeUyen Pham ; **15 (hd) :** Excerpt from the top-secret journal of Fiona Claire Jardin by Robin Cruise. Copyright © 1998 by Roberta Ann Cruise. Reprinted by permission of Houghton Mifflin Harcourt Publishing Compagny. All rights reserved ; **16 (hd) :** The Perks of Being a Wallflower, 2012/Collection Christophel © 2011 Summit Entertainment ; **16 (md) :** The perks of being a wallflower/Simon & Schuster ; **17 (m) :** Paul Box/reportdigital. co.uk ; **21, 35, 53, 67, 81, 99 (bd) :** Alex Bellem/BBC Learning English ; **21 (md) :** Matilda by Roald Dahl and illustration by Quentin Blake/United Agent ; **23 (h1) :** Fotolia ; **23 (h2) :** Milan Lipowski/Fotolia ; **23 (h3) :** dianazh/Istock ; **23 (mg) :** Audrey Lamy ; **24, 102 (hd) :** Diary of Wimpy Kid «Wimpy Kid Do It Yourself Book» by Jeff Kinney (first published in the US by Harry N Abrams, 2007, Puffin Books 2008) © Jeff Kinney, 2007 ; **25 (b1) :** ZaharovEvgeniy/stock ; **25 (b2) :** The Twits by Roald Dahl and illustration by Quentin Blake/ United Agent ; **27, 4(b)** JEWEL SAMAD / AFP ; **28 (bg) :** Alexander Raths/Fotolia ; **29 (hd1) :** timurock/Istock ; **29 (hd2) :** The White House ; **29 (m) :** jenifoto/Istock ; **30 (hd) :** Hilary-Morgan Watt ; **30 (mg) :** The white house ; **32 (b) :** kirin_photo/Istock ; **35 (md) :** My Favorite Recipes ; **35 (mg) :** IgorZakowski/Istock ; **36 :** Keep Calm-o-Matic ; **37 (md) :** hollygraphic /123RF ; **37 (mg) :** olm26250/istock ; **39 (b1) :** posteriori/Istock ; **39 (b2) :** vichie81/Istock ; **39 (b3) :** Bliznetsov/Istock ; **41, 5(h)** © Laura Ashman for Book Aid International ; **42, 43, 135 :** The brillant world of Tom Gates by Liz Pichon/David Higham Assosciates ; **45(1), 47(4), 5(b)** The Royal Mint ; **45, 5(b) (2) :** duncan1890/Istock ; **46 (hg) :** Maria Toutoudaki/Getty Images ; **46 (hd) :** Annie Coghlan ; **47 (1) :** The Royal Mint ; **47 (2) :** The Royal Mint ; **47 (3) :** The Royal Mint ; **47 (bg) :** The Royal Mint ; **47 (hd) :** Jane Austen ; **47 (hg) :** King Harold is killed and the English turn in flight, detail from the Bayeux Tapestry, before 1082 (wool embroidery on linen) / Musée de la Tapisserie, Bayeux, France / Bridgeman Images ; **47 (md) :** Fototeca Gilardi/Getty Images ; **47 (mg) :** SCIENCE SOURCE/Getty Images ; **48 (h) :** BBC ; **48 (m) :** The Fire of London (colour litho), D'Achille, Gino (20th century) / Private Collection / Bridgeman Images ; **49 :** by John Higgin's/Royal mail ; **50 (hd) :** Jane Austen (1775-1817) illustration from 'Little Journeys to the Homes of Famous Women', published 1897 (engraving) (later colouration), English School, (19th century) / Private Collection / Photo © Ken Welsh / Bridgeman Images ; **53 :** David Cole / Alamy Stock Photo ; **55 :** King Harold is killed and the English turn in flight, detail from the Bayeux Tapestry, before 1082 (wool embroidery on linen) / Musée de la Tapisserie, Bayeux, France / Bridgeman Images ; **56 :** Liz Pichon/English Heritage/David Higham Associates ; **57 (b1) :** DrPAS/Istock ; **57 (b2) :** kickstand/Istock ; **59, 6(h)** Jacobs Stock Photography/Getty Images ; **60 (bd) :** Stefano Politi Markovina / Alamy Stock Photo ; **60 (h1) :** «A day in New York» JacksGap ; **60 (h2) :** janaluchenko/ Fotolia ; **61 (g) :** «Courtesy of Lovely Streets (www.lovelystreets.com)» ; **61 (md) :** trappy76/Istock ; **62 (hg) :** Kevin Foy / Alamy Stock Photo ; **62 (hd) :** CameraonTV ; **63 (hd) :** ©Caitlin Ochs/The New York Times-REDUX-REA ; **63 (hg) :** ©Caitlin Ochs/The New York Times-REDUX-REA ; **67 (hd) :** Twin Design/Shutterstock ; **68 (md) :** Gordon Gurvan/ Cartoonstock.com ; **69 (hd1) :** SlocumMedia/Istock ; **69 (hd2) :** deimagine/Istock ; **69 (hd3) :** ChrisHepburn/Istock ; **69 (hd4) :** Sam Spiro/Fotolia ; **69 (hd5) :** ossiridian/123RF ; **71 (bd) :** mattjeacock/Istock ; **71 (bg) :** red_frog/Istock ; **71 (bm) :** S.Borisov/Shutterstock ; **73, 172, 6(b)** Raphael Lacoste/© 2013 Ubisoft Entertainment. All Rights Reserved. Assassin's Creed, Black Flag, Ubisoft, and the Ubisoft logo are trademarks of Ubisoft Entertainment in the US and/or other countries. ; **74 :** HorenkO/Shutterstock ; **74 (bd) :** macrovector/123RF ; **74 (bg1) : Сергей Тряпицын/**123RF ; **74 (bg2) :** Luseen Leiber/istock ; **74 (bg3) :** ivan mogilevchik/Fotolia ; **74 (hg) :** Vladimir Velichko/123RF ; **74 (md) :** Steven Belledin/MK3 International ; **75 (bg) :** Sitade/Getty Image ; **75 (hg) :** © Mary Evans/Rue des Archives ; **75 (m1) :** Antiques & Collectables / Alamy Stock Photo ; **75 (m2) :** horiyan/Shutterstock ; **75 (m3) :** Iakov Filimonov/123RF ; **77 (bd) :** BSWToy.com ; **77 (h) :** Pan, 2015/Berlanti Productions/Warner Bros Pictures/Collection Christophel ; **78 (bd) :** Magic Marks the spot - The very Nearly Honorable League of Pirates, 2013 by Dave Phillips/Harper Collins Publishers ; **78 (h) :** Pan, 2015/Berlanti Productions/Warner Bros Pictures/Collection Christophel ; **82 (bd) :** Carter, Jon/Cartoonstock.com ; **83 (hg) :** Pirates of the Caribbeans On stranger tides, 2011/Real Rob Marshall/Johnny Depp/Walt Disney Studios Motion Pictures France / Collection Christophel ; **84 (h) :** http://pirate.namegeneratorfun.com/ ; **85 (b1) :** etiennevoss/Istock ; **85 (b2) :** JerryPDX/Istock ; **87 :** Droits reservés (DR) ; **88, 7(h) «**King Arhtur excalibur Unsheathed» by Jeff Limke, illustrations by Thomas Yeates. Copyright © 2007 by Lerner Publishing Group, Inc. Reprinted with the permission of Graphic Universe™, a division of Lerner Publishing Group, Inc. All rights reserved ; **89 (bd) :** magann/Fotolia ; **89 (hg, hd, hm) :** Harry Potter II et la chambre des secrets , 2002 /COLLECTION CHRISTOPHEL © WARNER BROS ; **91, 7(b)** Bloomberg/Getty Images/Softbank Robotics ; **92 (h1) :** Lucasfilm/20th Century Fox / The Kobal Collection / Aurimages ; **92 (h2) :** Lucasfilm/Bad Robot/Walt Disney Studios / The Kobal Collection ; **92 (h3) :** I ROBOT (2004)/Fox Searchlight Pictures/Collection Christophel ; **92 (h4) :** Wall-e, 2008 / COLLECTION CHRISTOPHEL © Walt Disney / Pixar ; **93 (bd) :** VCG/Getty Images ; **93 (h) :** Big Heros 6 © 2014 Disney/ Collection Christophel ; **95 (h) :** Julien Tromeur/Shutterstock ; **96 (hd) :** Gino's Premium Images / Alamy Stock Photo ; **96 (md) :** ABCya.com LLC ; **97 (h) :** Big hero 6, 2015 / Real Don Hall et Chris Williams /Collection Christophel © 2014 Disney ; **99 (bd) :** Brett Lamb/123RF ; **99 (mg) :** akg-images / ullstein bild / allOver ; **101 (mg) :** EPA/EVERETT KENNEDY BROWN/ MAXPPP ; **101 (mg1) :** WALL E, 2008 / real Andrew Stanton / COLLECTION CHRISTOPHEL © Walt Disney ; **101 (mg2) :** Transformers / 2007 /réal : Michael Bay / COLLECTION CHRISTOPHEL © Dreamworks / Paramount ; **103 (b3) :** ET-ARTWORKS/Istock ; **103 (b1) :** Samtoon/Istock ; **103 (b2) :** Lightguard/Istock ; **103 (b4) :** Floortje/Istock ; **105, 8(h)** Kayeri Akweks ; **106 (bd) :** The New York Public Library ; **106 (h) :** Elizabeth Riley/Grayhawk Perkins ; **107 (h) :** Allapattah, 2004 (acrylic on canvas), Cortada, Xavier / Private Collection / Bridgeman Images ; **116 :** Hotel Transylvania, 2013 / Real Genndy Tartakovsky/Collection Christophel © 2012 CTMG / Sony Pictures ; **117 :** Voodoo Girl/The Melancholy Death of Oyster Boy & Other Stories, Tim Burton, 1997/Faber & Faber ; **118 :** Miss Peregrine s home for peculiar children, 2016 / Real Tim Burton. Colletcion Christophel © Twentieth century fox film Corporation / Chernin Entertainment / Scope pictures ; **120 :** Miss Peregrine s home for peculiar children, 2016 / Real Tim Burton. Colletcion Christophel © Twentieth century fox film Corporation / Chernin Entertainment / Scope pictures ; **122 :** BBC ; **123 (bd) :** Mélanie Herment ; **123 (bg) :** Jose Luis Stephens/ GettyImages ; **125 (a1) :** oss1248/Istock ; **125 (a2) :** marekzatko/Fotolia ; **125 (a3) :** Ondrej Chvatal/Shutterstock ; **125 (b1) :** sborisov/Istock ; **125 (b2) :** Viacheslav Lopatin/ Shutterstock ; **125 (b3) :** Lady-Photo/Istock ; **125 (bg) :** Jose Luis Stephens/Getty Images ; **125 (c1) :** Vpommeyrol/Istock ; **125 (c2) :** underwaterstas/Fotolia ; **125 (c3) :** Stephen Frink/Getty Images ; **125 (d1) :** Timothy Stirling/Fotolia ; **125 (d2) :** Rebecca Schortinghuis/Getty Images ; **125 (d3) :** LarsPeterLundstroem/Istock ; **125 (e1) :** assja_sav/Fotolia ; **125 (e2) :** CQYoung/Istock ; **125 (e3) :** sirichai_asawalapsakul/Istock ; **125 (f1) :** Contrast / Oliver Behrendt/ullstein bild via Getty Images ; **125 (f2) :** simonkr/Istock ; **125 (f3) :** FreezingRain/Istock ; **126 :** Sherif A. Wagih (s.wagih@hotmail.com)/Getty Images ; **128 :** astrosystem/Fotolia ; **130 (b) :** www.englishcentral.com ; **130 (hd) :** © sissoupitch/ Fotolia ; **130 (hg) :** Phillip Hobbs-Andresen/123RF ; **131 :** The curious Incident of the dog in the night time by Mark Haddon/Aitken Alexander Associates ; **132 (bg) :** Because you'll Never Meet Me by Leath thomas/Bloomsbury Publishing ; **134 (b) :** Photographee.eu/Fotolia.com ; **137 (b) :** sata_production/Fotolia ; **138 (b) :** Glowimages/GettyImages ; **140 (bg) :** mutsMaks/Istock ; **140 (hd) :** Gurzzza/Istock ; **140 (hg) :** DEA / L. ROMANO / Getty Images ; **141 (mg) :** Sudowoodo/Istock ; **141 (bd) :** Droits reservés (DR) ; **142 (h) :** Park, W. B/Cartoonstock.com ; **144 (mg) :** Droits reservés (DR) ; **146 (bg) :** temniy/Istock ; **146 (hd) :** Alexandr Bognat/Fotolia ; **147 (bg1) :** Fotolia ; **147 (bg3) :** ChoochartSansong/ Istock ; **147 (bg2) :** trianide/Istock ; **147 (bg4) :** Nikiteev_Konstantin/istock ; **148 (hd) :** Alexandr Bognat/Fotolia ; **150 (hg) :** PinkPueblo/Istock ; **151 (hd) :** Groupe Fleurus, Paris 1997 «L'imagerie des sorcières et des fées» collection «L'imagerie»/Emilie BEAUMONT/François Ruyer - Colette David - Sophie Toussaint ; **154 :** Fotoholik/Shutterstock ; **164 :** mshch/Fotolia.

Références des textes :

14,19 (b) : Excerpt(s) from ALVIN HO: ALLERGIC TO GIRLS, SCHOOL, AND OTHER SCARY THINGS by Lenore Look, text copyright © 2008 by Lenore Look. Used by permission of Random House Children's Books, a division of Penguin Random House LLC. All rights reserved ; **15 (h) :** Excerpt from the top-secret journal of Fiona Claire Jardin by Robin Cruise. Copyright © 1998 by Roberta Ann Cruise. Reprinted by permission of Houghton Mifflin Harcourt Publishing Compagny. All rights reserved ; **16 (hg) :** Reprinted with the permission of MTV/Pocket Books, a division of Simon & Schuster, Inc. from THE PERKS OF BEING A WALLFLOWER by Stephen Chbosky. Copyright © 1999 by Stephen Chbosky. All rights reserved. ; **24,102 (hd) :** Diary of Wimpy Kid «Wimpy Kid Do It Yourself Book» by Jeff Kinney (first published in the US by Harry N Abrams, 2007, Puffin Books 2008) © Jeff Kinney, 2007 ; **25 :** The Twits - Plays for Children «Meet the Twits» by Roald Dahl,1980/David Higham Associates ; **29 (h) :** Obamas Dance to «Thriller» at white House Halloween Party by Korte, Gregory, oct 31,2016/USA TODAY/Pars International ; **31,33 (h) :** The white house for kids, A History of a Home, office and National Symbol by katherine L.House,2014/ Reprinted by arrangement with Susan Schulman Literary Agency and Chicago Review Press ; **42 :** The brilliant world of Tom Gates by Liz Pichon,2011/Scholastic/David Higham Associates ; **57 :** «Pepys : Fire of London» / BBC saturday drama ; **63,65 :** «What Makes a New York City Kids?» by Andy Newman, Oct. 21, 2016/Pars International/New York Times ; **71 :** New York, New York,Paroles de Fred Ebb – Musique de John Kander© 1977 EMI Unart Catalog Inc.Avec l'aimable autorisation d'EMI Catalogue Partnership France. Droits Protégés. ; **76,79 :** Magic Marks the spot - The very Nearly Honorable League of Pirates, 2013 by Caroline Carlson/Harper Collins Publishers ; **94 :** Elon university school of communications ; **110 :** The brilliant world of Tom Gates by Liz Pichon, 2011/Scholastic/David Higham Associates ; **116 (h) :** My Hippo Has the Hiccups «I think my dad is Dracula» by Kenn Nesbitt, 2009/Sourcebooks Jabberwocky ; **117 (h) :** Voodoo Girl/The Melancholy Death of Oyster Boy & Other Stories by Tim Burton, 1997/Faber & Faber ; **118 :** "Miss Peregrine's Home for Peculiar Children" Copyright © by Ransom Riggs.Used by permissions. all rights reserved/Quirk Books ; **131 (md) :** The curious Incident of the dog in the night time by Mark Haddon, 2004/Aitken Alexander Associates ; **136 :** The Usborne, Write your own story book by Louie Stowell and Jane Chisholm, 2011/Usborne.

DR : Malgré nos efforts, il nous a été impossible de joindre certains photographes ou leurs ayants droit, ainsi que les éditeurs ou leur ayants droit pour certains documents, afin de solliciter l'autorisation de reproduction, mais nous avons naturellement réservé en notre comptabilité des droits usuels.

The English-speaking world

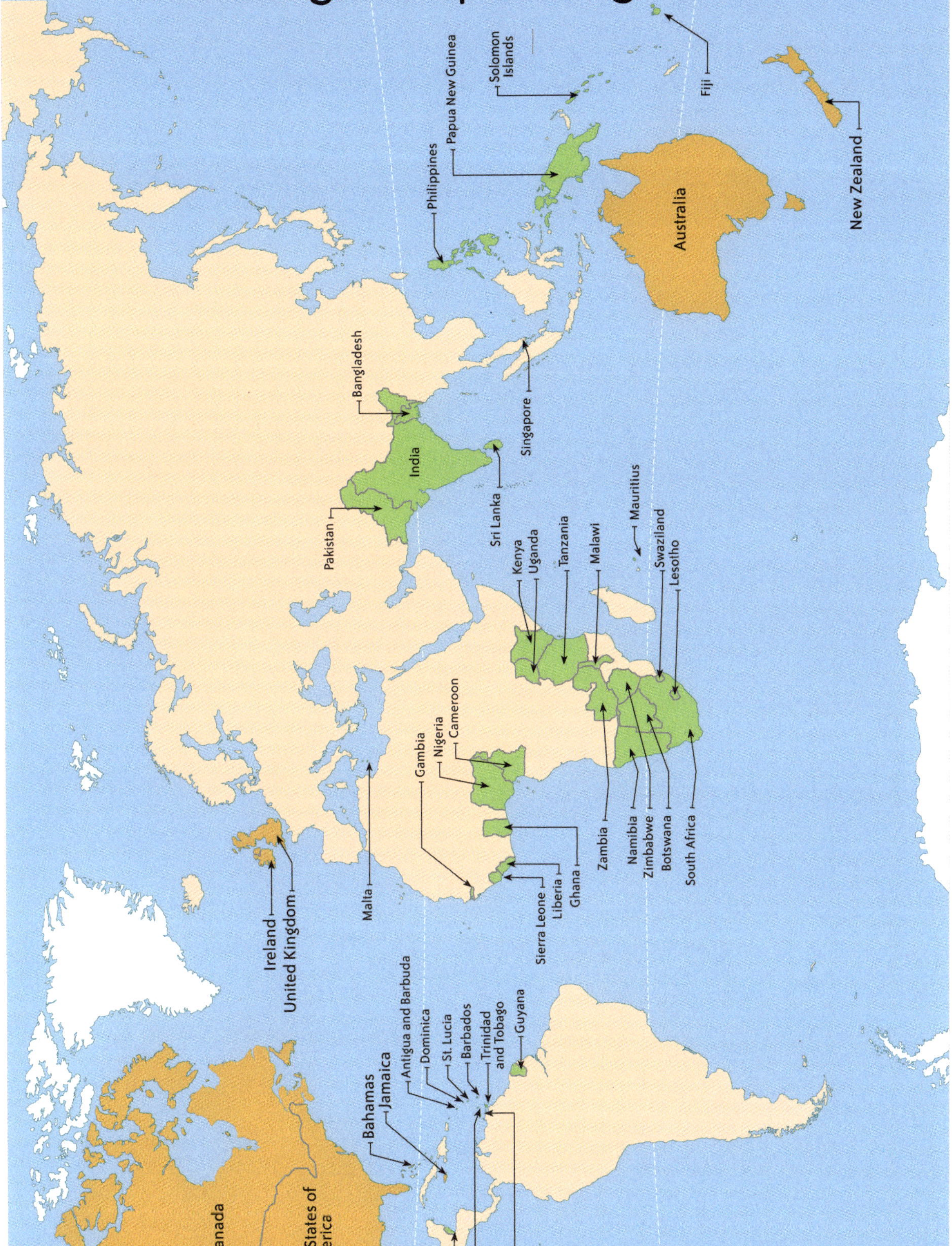

The British Isles